M000033442

5

GOD WILL DO
THE REST

GOD WILL DO THE REST

o—⚷

7 Keys to the Desires of Your Heart

Catherine Galasso-Vigorito

NEW YORK   BOSTON   NASHVILLE

The identities and details about some individuals in this book have been changed.

Copyright © 2009 by Catherine Galasso-Vigorito
All rights reserved. Except as permitted under the U.S. Copyright Act of 1976, no part of this publication may be reproduced, distributed, or transmitted in any form or by any means, or stored in a database or retrieval system, without the prior written permission of the publisher.

Scripture quotations noted NIV are from the Holy Bible, New International Version®. Copyright © 1973, 1978, 1984 by International Bible Society. Used by permission of Zondervan Publishing House. All rights reserved.   •   Scripture quotations noted NLT are from the *Holy Bible*, New Living Translation, copyright © 1996, 2004. Used by permission of Tyndale House Publishers, Inc., Wheaton, Illinois 60189. All rights reserved.   •   Scripture quotations noted NKJV are from the New King James Version. Copyright © 1982 by Thomas Nelson, Inc. Used by permission. All rights reserved.   •   Scripture quotations noted KJV are from the King James Version of the Holy Bible.   •   Scripture quotations noted NASB are from the New American Standard Bible®. Copyright © 1960, 1962, 1963, 1968, 1971, 1972, 1973, 1975, 1977, 1995 by The Lockman Foundation. Used by permission.   •   Scripture quotations noted RSV are from the Revised Standard Version of the Bible. Copyright © 1965 and 1966 by the Division of Christian Education of the National Council of the Churches of Christ in the U.S.A. Used by permission.   •   Scripture quotations noted TLB are from *The Living Bible*, copyright © 1971. Used by permission of Tyndale House Publishers, Inc., Wheaton, Illinois 60189. All rights reserved.

FaithWords
Hachette Book Group
237 Park Avenue
New York, NY 10017

Visit our Web site at www.faithwords.com.

Book design by Fearn Cutler de Vicq

Printed in the United States of America

First Edition: July 2009
10 9 8 7 6 5 4 3 2 1

FaithWords is a division of Hachette Book Group, Inc.
The FaithWords name and logo are trademarks of Hachette Book Group, Inc.

Library of Congress Cataloging-in-Publication Data

Galasso-Vigorito, Catherine.
    God will do the rest : 7 keys to the desires of your heart / Catherine Galasso-Vigorito—1st ed.
        p. cm.
    ISBN 978-0-446-54569-3
    1. Success—Religious aspects—Christianity.   I. Title.

BV4598.3.G35   2009
248.4—dc22
                    2008043387

To my husband, Todd:
For your unconditional love,
loyal, unwavering support, and gentleness of heart,
I dedicate this book to you.

And to our three daughters:
Lauren Grace
You are a treasure from God,
and I see myself in you in so many ways.
With your kind heart and multitude of talents,
limitless possibilities are ahead for you.
Gabriella
Your innate wisdom is astounding.
And your thoughtfulness and compassion are divine.
God gave us an angel in you, my dear child.
Sophia
You are a joy, the light of our lives,
and you will always be
my best friend.

May these "keys" give you the courage
to make all your God-inspired dreams come true.
I love you.

Contents

Acknowledgments

The LORD appeared . . . , saying:
"I have loved you with an everlasting love;
I have drawn you with loving-kindness."

—Jeremiah 31:3 NIV

Behind every dream is a dream team, for worthwhile accomplishments are never achieved alone.

With my heartfelt thanks and appreciation, I wish to acknowledge the following extraordinary individuals:

Claire Gerus, my gifted collaborator, literary agent, and dearest friend. Your genuine warmth, loving guidance, creative energy, and true friendship have blessed my life.

Ann Marie Brennan, my trusted friend, whose constant love, steadying influence, and unfailing faith in God has encouraged me onward.

Michelle Rapkin, my God-ordained executive editor. Words cannot express my admiration and appreciation to you for your unsurpassed creativity, wonderful instincts, graciousness, and compassion. Og is smiling down on us!

Holly Halverson, editor, FaithWords. You have a caring, generous heart. I am grateful for your loving touches and attention to every detail. It is wonderful working with you.

My extended family at Hachette Publishing Group, Inc., especially Senior Vice President/Publisher Rolf Zettersten and Associate Publisher of Editorial, Harry Helm.

I am privileged to work with such fine and dedicated people. Thank you for embracing me so warmly and enthusiastically. Additional thanks to:

Bill and Ruth Rush for giving me an opportunity for which I will be forever grateful.

Edward S. Condra, publisher, Jack Kramer, editor, and Richard Sandella, features editor, all of the *New Haven Register*, for your ongoing support.

John and Ruth Gibson for your outstanding example of godly character and dedication to the Lord. We are blessed to share our lives with you both.

Raymond and Julie Cirmo, I'm grateful for your love, wisdom, and constant encouragement.

Kim McHenry, your bright, vibrant personality always puts a smile on my face. Thank you for your love and for inspiring me to go farther.

Gia Calistro, I am thankful your optimistic outlook, for your faithfulness, and for your unwavering loyalty and friendship.

Kitty and Tom Law, I appreciate your sense of humor, sound advice, and the special bond we share.

Julie Foulk, many thanks for your continuous positive spirit, persistence, and sincerity of purpose.

Mary Campbell, Amy Corey, Jenne Frankelton, and Christine Palantino of QVC for your kindness and belief in me.

Michelle Cretella for your amazing enthusiasm, and Rebecca Malazzi for your fantastic sense of motivation.

Scott Taylor . . . I appreciate your wisdom and keen insights.

Maria Tannoia, Maryellen Taddei, William Cugno, Elizabeth Landow, Marshall Klein, Vincent Farricelli, the Emerson family, and the Marcus family—God has blessed me enormously with wonderful people like you.

Leo Tracey, Lori Labrie, Kevin Hurley and the staff at Cathedral Art Metal, Penny and Jim Martin of the Holy Land Stone Company, Diane and Dave Thompson of Bee Lieve Company, Bob and Skeeter Harju of Pumpernickel Press, Carol Hack of Gregg Gift Company, Edward Weiner of Maryland China, Aaron Bond of Books of Love, and Alena Margolis of Hartstrings, for your talents, enthusiasm, and gracious support. What an honor it is for me to be acquainted with such exceptional people and excellent organizations who share my vision to give glory to God and help people through extraordinary products of inspiration.

Lucille Clancy, Frank Clancy, Thomas Draicchio, and the late Renee Vigorito for your love so generously given.

To the readers of my newspaper column, *A New You*, thank you for your heartwarming letters, faith-filled stories, and words of encouragement. I appreciate you immensely and I am praying for you.

And to all the precious individuals who reached out to me with helping hands to lift me up when I was down, I will be eternally grateful. This book has been a gift to me, and I hope it will be a gift to you as well.

My greatest gratitude is to the Lord, for making this book and my dreams possible. And I pray that He will continue to direct me to do His will so I can continue to serve you in His name.

The Key to the Kingdom of Heaven Is Also Our Key to Happiness on Earth

A dear friend once told me that I am giving to others what I need the most. Those words rang true then and continue to ring true today. What began as a simple idea—to share with others the inspiration that helped me overcome my own challenging times—has become my life's mission.

As I write this book, I am humbled by the opportunity that I have been given: to impart to you the same seven keys—faith, persistence, optimism, hope, gratitude, love, and forgiveness—that have shaped my daily life, and to help you achieve the very best, your own heart's desires, in your precious time here on earth.

I know, all too well, how words of encouragement, given at just the right moment, can save a life . . . because they saved mine.

Could it be that more than twenty years have passed since the fateful morning that changed my life? Although time has rushed by, it is still difficult for me to write this, and my computer screen blurs as tears fill my eyes.

One late evening in the spring of 1987, I had just returned home from a friend's house. Earlier that afternoon, I had appeared in my hometown's Memorial Day parade. Only six weeks earlier, I had been crowned Miss Connecticut, USA, and I was feeling on top of the world.

As I walked into our kitchen to get a glass of water, I heard a noise behind me. Turning, I saw my mother approaching me.

"Oh, you startled me," I said as I turned toward her, happy to see her.

Mother was caring and kindness at its best. As a child, I always felt her love surround me, and even when I grew up, she cuddled me when no one else did. She had the gentlest heart I have ever known, and to me she was a living example of generosity and inner beauty. Relying on her faith in God, she lived life with grace and dignity. I remember her smile most of all, for she was always full of joy and happiest with a life of simple pleasures.

That night, for some reason, she seemed oddly weak and fragile. But I dismissed the thought and we talked a bit before I headed upstairs to my bedroom. Mother followed and told me her plans for the next day. Again I thought, *She looks so frail. . . .*

In retrospect, I wonder if God was trying to tell me something. But there was no reason to question her good health. Her eyes were bright and shining with her usual tenderness and affection.

I recalled, weeks before, that she had gazed often at me with a look of contemplation . . . maybe of unease. What was in that look? Was there love in her eyes? Yes, always. Was there concern for me? Most definitely.

Now, looking back, I believe she sensed that her time on earth was fast concluding. That dim May evening was the last time I saw my mother alive. The next morning when I walked down the hallway, I cautiously entered my mother's bedroom. There I found her, lying still and unresponsive, her breath silenced forever.

The word *devastated* cannot begin to describe how I felt upon the sudden loss of my mother and best friend. There were moments that I doubted I could even breathe. But there would be more.

Only one week after the funeral, I was forced to leave the only home I had ever known with barely the clothes on my back.

That could have been the beginning of a bitter and discouraged approach to life. But for me, survival would come in the form of heaven-sent inspiration.

My mother was close beside me as I entered the most traumatic period of my life. I felt her presence constantly as she guided me to the Bible to seek comfort and inspiration during those darkest of years.

Gratefully, I filled my mind with God's affirmative and life-giving promises, which helped me prevail as I pored over the Scriptures and inspirational books. Often I would delight in stories about men and women who had triumphed over adversity, drawing ever closer to God's light.

Gradually, these stories began to heal my heart. I learned that the secret to getting through life's challenges is not what happens to you, *but what you do with what happens*. The way we respond to what occurs will determine whether we will open the door to God's grace, doing what we can and leaving the rest to Him—or leave it tightly closed.

As I persevered, trying to create the right open door for me, I felt an inspiration: to help other people. I thought, *If encouraging, hopeful words helped me survive, then they can surely help others.* I wanted to share messages of hope with men and women who, like me, were seeking strength, direction, and courage.

When I became a syndicated columnist, I found myself writing of experiences we all share of both the spirit and the heart. It has been the greatest blessing for me to have received, over the past fifteen years, thousands of beautiful letters from worldwide readers of my columns and the book that followed.

These moments of sharing have brought me an overflow of joyful stories from other lives lifted up from despair and enriched by encouraging words and stories. It has delighted me to see how others have opened themselves to the love and faith hidden deep within them.

Regardless of the present or future challenges they face, these men and women are grateful for every breath they have been given. And with each breath, they are giving thanks for the bright future that awaits them.

Although I would not choose to relive those dark days of long ago, I do give thanks for them, recognizing that they were a test God had set before me. Today, I have a loving husband, three delightful daughters, and work that inspires me and gives hope to others.

Our magnificent Lord has wondrous plans for your life, too, and I am here to help you unlock those treasures within. All you need do is take each one of the seven keys to your heart's desires and unlock the storehouse of the Lord's riches that await you.

And what is the source of this treasure? It is one of the best gifts of all—the strength and faith that allow us to accept every experience as for our good, no matter how it first appears. As Romans 8:28 states, "We know that all things work together for good to those who love God, to those who are the called according to His purpose" (Romans 8:28 NKJV).

Today, the times of change and challenge we face require more faith than ever before. When we support and uplift others, even in small ways, we are serving God. I rejoice in the Scripture that says, "I tell you the truth, whatever you did for one of the least of these brothers of mine, you did for me" (Matthew 25:40 NIV).

Like an old-fashioned lantern, the Word of God guides us as we take one step at a time. He sheds His light on the paths of our lives—a light of pure love, wisdom, and grace. Step-by-step, day after day, and year after year, the joy of the Lord grows brighter and brighter as we approach our home in His kingdom. Now, with these seven keys in hand, we can unlock the secrets to a life ablaze with the spirit of His love—right here on earth.

Blessings,

Catherine

Catherine

I know thy works: behold, I have set before thee an open door, and no man can shut it: for thou hast a little strength, and hast kept my word, and hast not denied my name.

—Revelation 3:8 KJV

GOD WILL DO
THE REST

Key #1:
FAITH

I tell you the truth, if you have faith as small as
a mustard seed, you can say to this mountain,
"Move from here to there" and it will move.

(Matthew 17:20 NIV)

I have learned that there is a Force beyond what we can see . . . and that a Supreme Power is at work in our lives.

Although we may have been cast upon the turbulent seas of life, if we have faith, God will guide us to a peaceful harbor.

I have found that at the most challenging times, when I call on my faith the obstacles before me begin to move aside, and I can move forward with renewed hope.

With faith in God and in ourselves, we can open the doorway to boundless possibilities, new opportunities, and limitless power. Faith is like radar that sees through a temporary fog, and when we realize that our "radar" is working, our hearts are lifted and our fears melt away.

Together, dear readers, let us take the next step toward finding our faith, for when we do, we will discover that . . .

- ❦ on the other side of defeat, there is victory.
- ❦ on the other side of failure is success.
- ❦ on the other side of turmoil is peace.

Even the smallest amount of faith is enough for God. He will not only guide us, but He will walk beside us on our journeys. With God as our Divine Partner, nothing shall be impossible for us. For He is the Author of our lives, and His loving plan will ultimately bring us to victory.

HAVE FAITH AND YOUR HEART'S DESIRE WILL COME TO PASS

Sometimes, all we need is a little faith . . .

- ❧ faith that we will overcome a situation.
- ❧ faith that we will achieve our hearts' desires.
- ❧ faith that we will survive.

God speaks clearly of the power of faith. He reveals that if we have faith even as small as a grain of mustard seed, nothing will be impossible for us. He tells us that our faith can move mountains. And He shows that our faith can achieve the impossible when it is His perfect will.

Many times we think that we must *see* it to believe it, but God says you have to *believe* it, and then you'll see it. And I have found that this is indeed the way things work.

- ❧ Before I purchased my first car, I bought a decorative front license plate. I told myself that it would adorn the white automobile that I *imagined* I would own.
- ❧ Before I owned a home of my own, I purchased a lovely angel lithograph that I *anticipated* I'd place in the foyer of my new dwelling.
- ❧ Before I met my husband, I listed the attributes I was looking for in the man I *hoped* to one day marry.
- ❧ Before I began writing my newspaper column, I joyfully *visualized* the people it would help.

Sometimes we must work from the end to the beginning, imagining, believing, and anticipating the good aspirations we desire. Then our focused minds will help our goals to manifest. *Seeing and results*

(True faith means believing in what you do not yet see, and the reward of having great faith is to actually *see* what you so strongly believed to be true) I like what American philosopher and poet Ralph Waldo Emerson wrote: "All I have seen has taught me to trust the Creator for all I have not seen."

I have followed this principle my entire life, and I have been amazed by the results. Moreover, when I have faith not only in myself, but in God and His ability to work through me, I have seen the extraordinary occur!)

As I sit here this morning with a clean white sheet of paper and a pencil in my hand, I translate invisible thoughts into actual words, unseen reflections into reality, the intangible into the concrete. As my thoughts flow onto paper, I rejoice that God has sown His seeds of hope and joyful expectation into my mind and heart, so that I can share them with others.

I have learned to expect that His Word will flow through me when I open myself to His loving voice, and as I read what I have written and see the effect these words have on others, I am humbled and grateful.

Similarly, when you expect faith to work, you can rest assured that what you seek will, in God's time, happen. You can be certain that if it is God's divine will, what you work and hope for will be awaiting you, even if you cannot see it up ahead.

Now it is time to step forward into the fullness of His plan and achieve your destiny. Believe in your unique, very special gifts. Set your sights high. Discover your inner strength and you will determine your own worth, because with God as your partner, nothing is impossible.

Can you envision your dream? Then you can achieve it.

Can you see yourself accomplishing your goals? Then you will!

One afternoon, I asked my daughter Lauren what the word *faith* means to her. My nine-year-old confidently replied, "When I hear the word *faith*, I think of it as someone believing they can do anything."

Next I asked, "Can you give me an example?"

Lauren said, "Sure, Mom. For instance, if someone didn't do very well in a dance rehearsal, they would *expect* to do better the next time."

When you work with expectant, affirmative, and enthusiastic faith, when you say what you want and doubt not in your heart, you will watch in wonderment as the extraordinary occurs.

Therefore, *expect* this to be a fantastic day, *expect* your children to flourish, *expect* your relationships to thrive, *expect* good health, *expect* to overcome setbacks, and *expect* your business to succeed. What you expect, you'll attract. Expect the good, and it will be yours.

"Catherine, what else can I do?" you might question. Forget the "what-ifs." Never, ever look back. Negativity can delay the positive, so reprogram your mind to get rid of any lingering doubts or fears. If thoughts of failure seep into your thoughts, focus on the fact that God is in control. Recall that Psalm 62:7–8 declares, "In God is my salvation and my glory: the rock of my strength, and my refuge, is in God. Trust in him at all times" (Psalm 62:7–8 KJV).

Keep in mind: you are the living son or daughter of God. There is no greater protection than the assurance of God's love for you. Now, believe it and go forth with action—just as the centurion did during the time of Jesus.

In the Bible, Matthew chapter 8 tells us a story of faith in action. A centurion had heard about the miracles of Jesus, and he unquestionably believed that Jesus had the supreme power and authority to perform these wonders. When his servant became ill, the centurion approached Jesus to ask Him to heal this beloved member of the family.

The passage describes how Jesus told the centurion, "Go; it shall be done for you, as you have believed" (Matthew 8:13 NASB). And the centurion's servant was healed at that very moment. Though joyful at the outcome, the centurion was not really surprised. In fact, he fully expected to see his servant's health restored. He understood the basics of faith and took God's word as the answer he had sought.

For what was said to him is said to all of us: Believe, and you shall receive; only believe and see the power of faith.

IN TIMES OF TRIAL, LET GO AND LET GOD LEAD

The first line of a hymn says, "Prayer is the key to heaven, but faith unlocks the door" (Samuel T. Scott and Robert L. Sande).

I folded my hands in a tight embrace, looked to God, and prayed, "If this is Your will, Lord . . . if this is where You want me to be, just open the door and let me walk through. If it is not, then You can shut it tight and I'll walk away."

Five years ago, my husband, Todd, and I were having breakfast at a local restaurant. On the table was a real-estate booklet showcasing houses for sale. Casually I began looking through it. My eyes widened as I turned to the fourth page and saw a photo of a grand home under construction.

"Let's go and see this house," I urged Todd as I sipped my coffee. "It looks so beautiful."

The home reminded me of a photo that I had seen long ago in a magazine. About fifteen years earlier, when I lived in a tiny two-room apartment, I had cut out a photo of an author's gorgeous home and placed it in a decorating book, gazing at it from time to time.

That very morning we called the Realtor, who gave us the address of the home. We drove down a long, winding country road, following the directions, then took a left turn into the new development.

I looked to my right. The house was in a beautiful neighborhood, and it sat high on a slight hill, with two grand pillars placed at the front entrance. Although still unfinished, we could see that it would be breathtaking. We parked our car in the driveway and I said enthusiastically, "Let's go in!"

The construction workers were there, as well as the builder. We walked through each room, and I imagined what kind of curtains would adorn the windows, where my desk would be placed in the large home office, and how our children would one day play outdoors on the spacious two acres of land.

At first we both thought the house was beyond our reach. But because I trusted that the impossible can become possible, I asked Todd, "Can we run the numbers? Let's try. Maybe it could work."

Subsequently, after careful planning and consideration, we put down a deposit on the new construction, contingent upon the sale of our present home.

Well, it was one thing after another. Everywhere we turned, we met another stumbling block. Our current house wasn't selling; the builder needed to finish the customization of the house, and time was running out on our contract.

After much prayer, we decided that this was not where God wanted us. So we withdrew our deposit and walked away. Somehow, though, I just couldn't give up on my dream.

Week after week, we drove past the neighborhood. We continued to have faith and saw our dream home coming to pass in our minds. And one day, as we were parked in front of that house, Todd said to me, "Look across the street."

We had been so focused on the first house that we didn't even realize there was a lovely vacant lot right across the street!

"Let's make the developer an offer on that lot," Todd suggested. Soon after, we bought the lot quite reasonably, sold our previous home, contracted with a wonderful builder, and watched him build the home of our dreams.

It is a dwelling similar to the picture I cut out of that old magazine, the elegant home I imagined so many years ago. God is so good, and He always holds something better for us on the horizon.

I have learned to place everything in God's hands and leave the outcome of each situation to Him. He knows what my desires are, but most important, He knows what I need. I have come to believe that He has designed a life plan for me. When I follow His lead, I may encounter some obstacles, but ultimately, I arrive at a place of peace and joy.

Sometimes God gives us tests and watches carefully to see how we will respond. When we choose to pray and then give the situation back to Him to take care of, He will always bring about what's best for us.

When we put down our deposit on that new home under

construction and circumstances did not go our way, I began to experience great anxiety. But when I contemplated what to do, I remembered that the wisdom of God is first and foremost the wisdom of peace that brings us to fulfillment.

I stopped, listened, and trusted as I felt God wrap His peace and love around me. As my stress level evaporated, I became calm once again. I also clearly understood that when God wants something for us, He opens the door wide so that we can walk through. On the other side is His gift—the right gift—for us.

If you must constantly ask others, "What should I do?" you would be wise to await His guidance. You need not give up your plans, but if something or someone is causing you heartache or stress, turn to God and put your faith in Him to take care of it. A friend of mine recommends, "Say a prayer and put your hope in God. He will lead you the way He wants you to go."

At the same time, try to separate from those who disturb your peace of mind. When you are in a more peaceful place, you will be better able to hear His voice. When you are prayerful, you will become more sensitive to who and what is in your life. Sometimes a corner must be turned before a prayer can be answered. If this is the case, have faith that He will lead you to that corner.

God has told us, "Seek peace, and pursue it" (Psalm 34:14 KJV). Therefore, I carefully consider any situation that does not feel harmonious to me. Because the ways of the Lord are those of peace, strength, and goodness, those are the qualities I choose to experience.

One day, Susan, a friend, told me that the hours at her job had been severely cut back and her boss was giving her a difficult time. Although she was close to despair, she chose to pray for help, to put her problems in God's hands. The very next week, Susan discovered five hundred dollars in a dresser drawer she had forgotten about. Soon afterward, she learned that her troublesome manager was being transferred to another location. Suddenly, everything was going her way!

"God always takes care of me," Susan told me happily. And I agree! He is no respecter of rank or station but will do His loving work for any one of us. He asks only that we reach out to Him, and that we have faith in Him to deliver.

When you do so, you will discover a wonderful secret: He is in control, His ways are best, and His plans are glorious. When He says, "Do not worry, My child, I will supply your needs," rest assured that He will carry your burdens when you ask Him to do so.

It is good to know that God's guidance will light our pathways through life. Keep in mind, "He is always thinking about you and watching everything that concerns you" (1 Peter 5:7 TLB).

PEOPLE MAY JUDGE US BY OUR SUCCESSES, BUT GOD LOOKS ONLY AT OUR EFFORTS

When you march into the open arms of faith and take a step into the unknown, you must trust that one of two things will happen: either a clear path will appear for your journey, or God's hand will guide you to find it.

It is easy to persevere and have faith when things are going well, but what makes us overcome our limitations and rise to new levels of success? The answer is this: being able to recognize opportunities when we encounter adversity.

I admire the faith-filled attitude of a business colleague of mine. He recently told me that he was on the verge of losing his biggest client. However, instead of being worried or upset, he said, "I know if this doesn't work out, God has something better for me. More and better opportunities are just ahead."

And he was right. For the client he lost, two new ones appeared within weeks who were easier to work with and whom he could bring to greater success. Once again, my friend's faith was rewarded, and I was newly inspired by his story.

I recall a conversation I had with a young lady who said, "Catherine, I have a challenging situation at work with a difficult new boss. How can I keep faith during this time?"

I pointed out that many who have faced such challenges report that adversity brought with it surprising gifts. So when hardship comes, summon the courage to push forward.

In the Bible, I read that there was a woman who, for twelve years, endured much pain and suffering with an illness that caused continual bleeding. She had undergone many different treatments for her illness without even a glimmer of healing. Still, she rose above her fears with great faith, and with it she reached out to touch the hem of Jesus' robe. She believed, "If I just touch his clothes, I will be healed" (Mark 5:28 NIV).

So she did not give up and worked her way through the crowds until she came up just behind Him. Then she reached out her hand and touched the edge of His cloak. Immediately, her bleeding stopped.

Jesus asked, "Who touched me?" But no one knew. But Jesus felt "that power had gone out from him" (Mark 5:30 NIV). Then the woman fell at His feet, told why she had touched Him, and explained how she had been instantly restored to health.

I love the words Jesus spoke: "Daughter, your faith has made you well; go in peace, healed of your disease" (Mark 5:34 TLB).

At times, to leave adversity behind you must go through it. There may be twists, turns, and valleys on your path, but the Spirit of God will lead you to victory. Think of setbacks as teachers sent to help you build knowledge, strength, and endurance.

Often problems hold their own solutions. When we have faith, we look forward to a successful outcome. By believing in God's promises, we will see things work out, often better than we might imagine. We will triumph over our problems if we approach them with faith in God and the power of our prayers.

This brings to mind the letter a fifty-five-year-old reader of my column wrote to me six years ago. He revealed that he had suffered serious medical problems and as a result had lost his business and almost everything he owned. But instead of giving up, he remained optimistic about the future, and when he was able to regain his strength, he started another business.

Starting over with ongoing health issues seemed almost impossible, but this man remained steadfast and strong by counting his blessings and recalling the incredible things God had done for him in the past.

A short time ago, I received another letter from him. He enthusiastically affirmed that his health had dramatically improved, his new company was doing well, his home life was happier, and his son was working with him in the family business. He praised God for transforming his circumstances and giving him a fresh start.

Everyone has a purpose in life. If you have breath in your body, it means you still have goals to accomplish. The goal God best recognizes is the one that will help and uplift another, so persist in your goal of making the world a better place. God blesses those who endure and who help others do the same.

SURRENDER AND BECOME WHAT GOD CREATED YOU TO BE

I guess I wanted to read it in the sky, as if written by a sky-writing airplane—an affirmation of what I should do. Seeking a reassuring voice, I tried to clearly hear the answer I was searching for.

Am I making the correct decision? I questioned myself. *Is this the right thing to do?*

It was the spring of 2005, and I was recuperating from the difficult birth of my third daughter, Sophia. Sitting in my home office, I was reading letter after letter from readers of my newspaper column.

"I just wanted to let you know you are blessing my life," one reader wrote. "God led you to the work you do by helping thousands of people who are troubled, lost, or just need inspiration."

"You certainly got through to me," e-mailed another.

"If I am down, your newspaper columns pick me up and inspire me. It leaves me with new hope and a feeling that everything will be okay," said one more.

"Your articles have been of great encouragement to me and my husband. Thank you for allowing God to use your talents to minister to others."

And often I read, "Thank you, Catherine. . . . I feel as though you were writing this just for me."

Through the years, I have received thousands of beautiful letters from teenagers, mothers, fathers, soldiers, cancer survivors, businessmen, school superintendents, corrections officers, naval sub-mariners, firemen, the elderly, nurses—people from all walks of life.

But something within me was still not complete. *How else can I help people?* I wondered. *How can I make a difference in more people's lives?*

As I sat with my three-month-old baby contently cradled in my arms, I gazed outside my office window at the peacefulness of nature. The light came streaming in through the burgundy-and-gold-fringed curtains, and a glow diffused through the room. Suddenly I sensed something come over me.

I felt a *calling*, as I like to describe it, and I knew that there was indeed something else for me to do.

For the previous twelve years, while writing my weekly inspirational column, I had been working in radio advertising. I loved the job and my clients but often wondered if that was where God wanted me to stay.

That day, as I reflected and was still, I could listen to His voice in my heart . . . and yes, there was something else for me to do.

So in obedience I prayed, "What else can I do to help, Lord? I turn my heart's desire over to You. It is in Your mighty hands. You decide."

I felt inspired, at that moment, to reach over for my Bible and open it at random. The pages fell to Jeremiah 27:12 and my eyes fell upon seven words: "Serve him and his people, and live!" (Jeremiah 27:12 NKJV).

Those seven words have moved me forward when I questioned my path. And dear reader, if you are confronted with a difficult decision, take time to seek God's voice, and listen to the echoes of His will in your own God-inspired thoughts. Then, faithfully follow your heart, allowing yourself to be what God intended you to be.

Shortly after this experience, with Todd's support and one click of my computer mouse, my shaking right hand hit the Send button and I resigned from the world of advertising. I would pursue my dream of sharing inspiring thoughts and products with others on a full-time basis.

With our newly calculated household budget in place, I gave up a large salary, an expense account, awards, benefits, my 401(k), and the luxuries that went along with the position, to stay home with our three young children and follow God's lead.

Todd assisted me when he came home from work, and together at our kitchen table we joined together to develop a new business. We created business plans, built a Web site, designed an entire product line complete with artwork, and brainstormed plans for manufacturing, bookkeeping, and marketing. It was a monumental task!

During that first three-year period, we were called to make countless sacrifices; there were struggles and stumbling blocks. Often I would call my dear friend, Ann Marie, for much-needed support.

"Forget the pain of the past month. Look forward with the Lord's help to success and happiness," she would reassure me.

When I hit a huge obstacle, she would advise, "Everything will be fine. Just when it looks the darkest, the clouds will part and the sun will come through. Trust in Him."

Day after day, week after week, Ann Marie would encourage me, "Let's keep praying and keep forging ahead." And after a major setback, she wrote me, "Catherine, you will come out of this a better person," and "God has a plan for you—you just have to let Him lead the way."

After that, I realized I would put everything in God's hands, and whatever He wanted for me, I would accept as His will. Subsequently, when I went through a tough situation that I did not understand, I actually visualized the Lord setting up His plan on my behalf. When I stumbled, I would picture the Lord's hands helping me stand up and try once again. And when one door closed, I remained optimistic and persisted, believing that God would one day, in His perfect timing, open a better door to new opportunities.

We must remember this: God would never ask us to endure a trial without having a purpose behind it. Therefore, when we meet challenges with faith in God's promises, we can trust that He is guiding us to the proper path—to the desires He has placed in our hearts.

It is early morning, and as I work in my office preparing this book, I can't help but know God is with me and has been all along. All I needed was to have faith in Him, to know that His hand would guide me to this place.

"But Catherine, what should I do when I am faced with a crucial decision?" you may ask. Prayer is a powerful ally for us. If we weigh all our decisions with prayer, seeking God's will, we can assess what is really motivating us and recognize our true objectives. When the answer is not clear, have patience. Sometimes He has a better plan in store and is clearing the path of other parties who will be involved.

By heeding the advice of the One who knows all things, we can triumph over every obstacle and find peace. So believe in Him, and trust that good things will happen. And they will.

FAITH BRINGS US A SENSE OF SELF-WORTH

When I was younger, some people often made me feel unworthy of love. While walking alone around the high school track one day, I looked up and asked, "Lord, have You forgotten me?" A peace washed over me as God entered my heart and said, "I have not forgotten you. . . . I have plans for you. You have many gifts to offer that are uniquely yours, and I will guide you in how to use them."

My heart was suddenly filled with so much love that all I wanted to do was open up and give that love to others.

Today I have a clear vision of what I'd like to be and do, so I try to live as if this vision has already come to pass. By acting upon what I believe are God's plans for me, I can manifest outwardly the faith I have within my heart.

Such thoughts of faith can help events turn out the way I trust they should. I always create a mental snapshot of my goal (my heart's desire) and see myself as having already achieved it. It's one of the best ways I've found to motivate myself.

Each day, I promise myself to do one small thing as a step toward reaching my desired goal. I've learned that there is no task I can't handle if I break it up into little pieces! And with each task I accomplish, my belief in myself and my worthiness to work for our Lord is strengthened.

Nothing succeeds like success, and by expecting to succeed and then doing so, we will feel more love and more loving toward ourselves. From that place, we can share more love with those around us.

Others, in turn, will pass around more love to those they touch. What a wonderful bounty of love we can produce, one by one, just by expecting that with God's help, we will succeed in making our dreams come true!

From every walk of life, those who achieve worthwhile objectives use the power of their words and their minds to carry out meaningful endeavors. Your thoughts and words can bind you or free you, so choose those that will free you to soar rather than being earthbound by those of weakness.

Maybe you were told, "You're too old," or "You'll never achieve that goal." Nonsense! Your soul is eternally young, a reflection of an ever-youthful, vibrant spirit. Remove the mental kinks that are blocking creativity, and destroy that paralyzing word *can't*.

If you say, "I can't do that," or "I can't accomplish my ambitions," you will find that events support your belief. On the other hand, if you declare, "I will be successful," and "I am valuable," then you can create the very condition you desire.

God knows that when you say or hear something often enough, you will start to believe it. Accordingly, you must always think and declare words of victory.

That was the attitude of one dear reader who wrote that an accident left her unable to walk without assistance. She said encouraging words from my column inspired her to try to walk independently again. So, she reminded God of His ability to make a way out of no way and took a step. And the next day, another. Faith got her back on her feet!

Speak aloud the things that you desire. Repeat your requests over and over until they drop down from your mind into your heart and become perfect faith. Use your words of faith to transform your situation.

The Bible says, "All things for which you pray and ask, believe that you have received them, and they will be granted to you" (Mark 11:24 NASB). Listen to the voice within that repeats, "You can do it!" "You will succeed!" and silence the depression that says, "You won't" or "It's too late."

I believe God wants you to have unlimited success. Let Him know what you desire, whispering a prayer in your heart and developing a discipline of faith. Declare, "This is the plan I have. If it is God's will, I will not let any distractions stand in my way." Then keep moving in the direction of your God-inspired purpose. And be sure to do something every day, even if it's just for five minutes, that is a step toward attaining it.

I still recollect the countless times when critics told me, "You'll never make it" or "Give up," or made fun of my ambitions. I paid no attention, and with unwavering faith I found out I could achieve my heart's dream.

For well over fifteen years, I've kept a three-by-five card in my daily planner with a poem on it. The edges of the card have become worn and faded, but the poem's profound message continues to ring true. Grace E. Easley's "Lesson" talks about pressing on in spite of naysayers—and victory at the end of the road: "And I found to my amazement, at the ending of the day, that what they said I couldn't, I had managed anyway." The secret? Asking God to do what only He can.

Each time I read the poem, it is as if I perceive the sound of God's voice whispering in my ear, "He who began a good work in you will carry it on to completion" (Philippians 1:6 NIV).

Search your heart to find out what it is you truly desire. If you have a goal born from a love for others and the wish to glorify God, you will have all of heaven behind you!

And as I bow down before Him with a humble heart, I am

confident that whatever God begins in your life, no matter what dream He puts in your heart, He will complete it.

BE PATIENT—GOD HAS HIS OWN TIMETABLE FOR YOU

Remember the lines from the Lord's Prayer that say, "Thy Kingdom come. Thy will be done" (Matthew 6:10 KJV)? God knows what He wants to place in your hands. Therefore, your prayer must be, "God, lead me to what You desire for me." And keep in mind that God's timetable is one of the mysteries of life.

Sometimes it seems as if you are waiting and waiting, and that your prayers have not been heard. Not true! In fact, God is working things out on His own timetable, and in His infinite wisdom events must move in a certain order. That is why you must continue to believe that He will answer every prayer—in His perfect time.

On God's clock there are no hands, minutes, hours, or seconds, just the beating of a heart, ticking away in perfect love. Like clockwork, God's timing is always exact. God will give you all you need and desire, but the time is not in your hands, it is in His.

You must be patient in your quest. God often delays your plans on purpose. Do you have the patience to wait for His leadership? Do you have the fortitude to persist?

God is building within you the strength of character to succeed in all your endeavors. Do you have what it takes to win the victor's crown? Are you determined to wear it?

Taking that step out in faith can be a difficult thing to do. But

God has a plan for your life that is more rewarding than anything you can imagine. He wants His best for you, so before you can receive it, you must fully surrender to Him.

Because God loves us so much, He often guides us by planting His own exquisite vision in the barren soil of our hearts. Like a gardener, will you cultivate that tiny seed to grow into a grand tree? Will you allow God's dreams for your life to materialize? Can you permit God's will to become your own?

At this moment, you are one choice away from a new beginning, another path, unique experiences, a different direction, and a cornucopia of opportunities. . . . This is the time for divine fulfillment. Your life is a great gift for you to live joyfully—it is the most precious jewel in the universe—so do what sincerely makes you happy.

It may take time, but as we stay focused and positive and persevere, God will step in and do what we cannot. He has placed each one of us here for a specific mission. We all have gifts that differ according to the grace given to us.

Have faith in your own extraordinary competence. And remember this: the word *impossible* isn't in the Lord's vocabulary. The life that God intended you to have is one of joyful expectation and good cheer.

Be sensitive to God's exact timing. Many a time I have called my friend Kim to hear her exclaim with joy, "I can't believe you called me! I was just thinking of you." To me, this is evidence of God's ideal timing once again, for He is in the midst of everything we do.

Remember when you almost didn't go to that fateful meeting, but something spurred you onward and there you were inspired to begin your dream job? Or when you changed your plans and went to a gathering and met your soul mate? Were these chance occurrences?

Many a time God challenges us with a subtle happening and watches how we handle it. Because He has given us this power to choose, the way we react during these tests often determines our future course.

Believing in and following God's timetable brings us wonderful rewards. Here is a true story that testifies to one woman's faith when she gave her life over to God.

Julie is an exceptionally giving person, and she believed that God wanted her to enter a new business endeavor, a project where she could have a more positive impact on greater numbers of people. So, after sixteen years in a solid, stable career, she resigned from the company to follow the dream she felt God had placed in her heart.

The next two years were filled with countless struggles, frustrations, and obstacles. Finally she was granted a meeting with a businessman who could be very influential in her new career path. During this meeting, the gentleman kindly but quite firmly told her it would take at least three more years to achieve her goal.

Julie was terribly disappointed. "Three or four more years?" she said, distressed. "Catherine, I've already spent over two years of my life pursuing this dream." Because she was then in her forties, she calculated her current age plus four more years. Then she reflected on her young children, her home, and how much everyone in her family had already sacrificed.

Walking to her car that cloudy afternoon, Julie recalled that she questioned whether or not she should go back to her old job. But her faith told her to keep on trying. She did not let her mind talk her out of her dreams. Instead, she continued to work hard, visualized success, talked about her future achievements, and believed her God-inspired dream would come about. All the while, she prayed, "Lord, please keep me on track."

Exactly seven months later, my friend was offered the opportunity of a lifetime. The job of her dreams opened up and she took it, offering thanks to the One who said, "*All* things are possible" (Matthew 19:26, italics added). Once again, God had the final say, and it was good. Julie did her part, and God did His. The result was another "everyday miracle."

Even when it looks as if everything has turned upside down or is about to be lost, that's the time to say, "Thank You, God. I know You hold me in the palm of Your hand, and I know that in Your precise time, I will be victorious." Soon, as you keep pressing on in faith, you will see God's perfect plan revealed.

A reader of my newspaper column recently wrote that the challenges of life so overwhelmed her that she was tempted to give up on God. Instead of dissolving her faith in tears, though, she hung on. In time she saw God redeem so many of her struggles that she now affirms His unfailing love and comfort. God's clock, she noted, runs differently from ours, and we need to give Him time to do His transforming work.

Of course, the challenges of our daily lives can bring us down with an obstacle here, a frustration there. . . . But through them all, we need to remember that God is faithful to us. He can do far more than we could ever ask or think, and His realm of possibility is infinitely beyond our highest aspirations and prayers.

Is it chance that you are reading this book at this exact moment? God has allowed these words to appear to you today to put you on the right track, to turn you around to Him, and to lift you above earthbound ways of thinking. He reminds you that you are His creation, He is your Guide, and He has designed success for everything that you do.

In the morning, the sun rises to begin a fresh, new day and then sets in the cool of the evening. The warmth and illuminating rays of summertime vanish into the bitter cold of winter. Trees change shape and color, the leaves fall to the ground. And under the ice and snow, hidden from your sight, the life in the roots of the trees begins to rise again.

God's timing is precise. You, too, shall rise again after every experience you encounter, because your life and your time are in God's mighty hands.

DO WHAT YOU CAN AND GOD WILL
DO THE REST

It is 10:17 a.m., 10:18 a.m., 11:05 a.m. . . . My eyes keep gazing at the clock. A few more minutes pass as I sit in the silence of my office, waiting.

It has been the longest week of my life. I am waiting for a phone call about a project that I have been working on for years. If approved, it can help me share my messages of hope and faith with an even larger audience.

Some time ago, I became involved with one of the home-shopping channels. The leaders there expressed interest in bringing me and my inspirational product line to their network. This morning they are meeting to determine if we will move forward together.

God sometimes calls the weak, the least likely, and the unassuming. But with His strength, the weak can become strong, the unwanted can be propelled by a new chance, and the average can accomplish the remarkable.

Leaning back in my office chair, I think back on my long, faith-filled journey, in which every step has demanded clarity of vision, hard work, tremendous patience, supportive people, and courage.

Most important, however, there have been countless times when I needed a source of strength beyond myself. I found this source in my faith. I love the verses in Proverbs that read, "Trust in the LORD with all thine heart; and lean not unto thine own understanding. In all thy ways acknowledge him, and he shall direct thy paths" (Proverbs 3:5–6 KJV). This passage is framed and sits on my desk, and as I glance at it each day, it has become my daily prayer.

Often God uses our weaknesses to show His strength. I have heard doctors say that premature babies who fight to live seem to be stronger and healthier in the long run.

And remember how Peter attempted to walk on water? He learned that he had to take hold of God's strength and carry on in faith. When his faith began to founder and he saw great waves and heard howling winds, he began to sink.

This is a lesson for us all, isn't it? We can't listen to the howling winds of doubt or stare at what seem to be impossible tasks and expect to make it to our goal. We must know deep within that we are doing God's will and hearing His calling. Then, one step at a time, we can accomplish what in the beginning seemed out of the question. We just have to keep our eyes on Him.

I like to contemplate the mighty universe in which we live, the power in the winds and the waves of the sea. And He who holds the earth in the palm of His hand, who scatters the planets across the sky, will surely direct our steps for our good and His glory.

And so I take a deep breath and decide to leave the outcome of my venture onto America's TV screens with Him. I trust that all things work together for the good to those who love God and are called according to His purpose.

A few moments ago the phone rang. To my delight, I learned that I will launch my first one-hour show in two months. God has endorsed my new pathway to help and encourage others.

Often I tell my children, "When you have unshakable faith and an unselfish desire to help others, there is nothing you cannot accomplish or achieve." Scripture tells us, " 'Not by might nor by power, but by My Spirit,' says the LORD of hosts" (Zechariah 4:6 NKJV).

It will be by His Spirit that you will triumph over that obstacle. By His Spirit you can receive health and healing. And by His Spirit you shall achieve your heart's desire.

Our Creator loves us all dearly. Take into account that because He desires the best for you, when you follow your dreams, you follow Him. No matter how far-fetched your dream seems or how long it takes, there are no impossibilities. We may appear to be the least likely to succeed or seem to lack the resources, material possessions, or genius to do so. But I have found that with ordinary talent, extraordinary faith, and unwavering perseverance, any dream is within reach.

BE LIKE "THE LITTLE ENGINE THAT COULD"

Do you remember a children's book called *The Little Engine That Could*? This was the story of a small engine that tried and tried and never gave up until it pulled the train to its destination.

A very simple children's story holds the proven key to success. Like the little engine, you will find that your dreams come true when you stay on track and stick to your God-given purpose. Keeping at it gets results, for all real achievement requires time and tenacity. If you can reach up and hold on to God's miraculous gift of endurance despite any obstacles, you'll have harnessed the power of a champion.

Thus, never limit your vision for yourself or your future. Expand your thoughts and believe for big dreams. In order to think *I can*, you have to feed positive images into your mind, actual pictures of every single step of your success. If you use your imagination to worry, change it to picture the successful outcome of every problem. If you use your memory to remember your hurts and failures, change it to remember the sweet and beautiful moments of your life.

"In life," a mentor said, smiling, "you have to believe." So eliminate negative mind-sets. Stop making excuses, dwelling on problems, and thinking about what you cannot do. Instead, see yourself as strong, prevailing over obstacles and rising to new heights.

A while ago, Todd designed and created a small cascading waterfall and a pond in our backyard. Todd is an engineer by trade and is ingenious, so when I asked him if he could construct a pond for us he declared, "Sure, this will be a great project."

All spring and into summer, he worked on his creation. The

girls helped, too. And after he was finished, we added two little frogs and twenty-six baby fish to his handiwork. To the side we placed a little bench, and all around the pond we planted beautiful seasonal flowers. All of us absolutely love this spot in our backyard. And people tend to be drawn to it when they visit us.

What I find most fascinating is how, as the water continually streams down, blanketing the large, hard rocks, the rocks appear to form different textures and shapes. The continual flow of a gentle stream of water, week after week, month after month, can wear down even the mightiest stone.

When I watch the water cascade down, time and again I am reminded of a quote I like from William Shakespeare: "Much rain wears the marble."

Sometimes, because we all want to see results *now*, we give up on a dream that seems too difficult to achieve. But by observing the lessons of the water on the rocks, we can see how God affirms to us one of life's most important truths: with persistence we can triumph and make our way through all "impossibilities."

Therefore, be steadfast in pursuing your goals, even if you come upon what seems to be an immovable obstacle. Remember that, like the water, your continuing stream of faith can wear away the most impressive blockage.

At times you may be disheartened because things didn't turn out exactly as you had hoped. Still, you can always be confident that God is working out His perfect plan for you. When you begin to lose your faith or feel your persistence flagging, you can be heartened by Joshua, who said, "Do not be afraid, nor be dismayed, for the LORD your God is with you wherever we go" (Joshua 1:9 NKJV).

A few years ago, a friend and her husband launched a new product of an inspirational nature. Since she and her husband pursued this idea together, they also funded it. They took out a loan, did all the work themselves, overcame countless setbacks, and after two years the product was launched nationwide. Though the product was well received by the public, the going was slow.

It was a task that at times seemed unfeasible, but through it all, in the midst of difficulties, they persevered and remained faithful, knowing that God was in control of this endeavor.

Nevertheless, it was extremely challenging, especially when they thought about the money they had invested and the loan that needed to be repaid. But they crowded out their doubts with trust and their fears with faith, believing it would all work out for the best.

They told me they took comfort in Psalm 27:13–14, which says, "I would have lost heart, unless I had believed that I would see the goodness of the LORD in the land of the living" (Psalm 27:13–14 NKJV).

Just recently, my friend started another project with an international company and was given a monetary advance to begin the endeavor. Well, the amount she was given as an advance was the exact amount of money, to the very penny, of the loan she and her husband had taken to fund their original product. I was awestruck when she told me what happened.

If you are going through a difficulty, know that you are not alone. God is with you, He loves you, and He will carry you through. Have faith. Believe. And in the end, you will see how He can turn adversity into victory!

To stay on the road to success, set aside a definite time at the beginning of each day to give thanks and ask for guidance to the open door of God's will. This is the key to ultimate victory.

During your day, resolve to help someone in some small way, at least once in the morning and again in the afternoon. A thoughtful act of kindness, a token of generosity, or a few reassuring words will brighten another person's day. And good deeds will return in a miraculous way to create in you the supreme love that never fails, for these are God's acts and His ways.

At the end of the day, the last thing left in the subconscious feeds the soul all through the night. Let it be an act of putting into God's care any unsolved problem, for with the dawn's light will come the solution.

A friend sent me this via e-mail. I liked it so much, I'm passing it on, with love, to you.

> Happiness keeps you sweet
> Trials keep you strong
> Sorrows keep you human
> Failures keep you humble
> Success keeps you glowing
> But only God keeps you going!

Let us keep in mind that our loving God is not just up there, beyond the sky, but He is right here in our hearts, working miracles every day, every hour, every minute. And as we honor Him, nothing will be impossible.

FAITH IN GOD FREES US FROM DAILY WORRIES

Are you carrying the burdens of life on your shoulders?
Are you holding on to the weight of the past?

Are you weary from worry?

One evening, a mother put her six-year-old son to bed and returned to the kitchen. A few minutes later, she heard a slight sound, looked up, and saw her little boy standing pensively at the doorway.

"What is it?" the boy's mother asked him, seeing his sad face. "What's the matter?"

A small cry escaped from his lips as he ran over and snuggled close to her. Wiping a tear away, he said, "I'm afraid of going to my new school tomorrow."

"Everything will be just fine," she assured him. "Leave it in Mommy's hands, all right?"

Reassured, the child nodded and let his mother walk him back to his room. She gently kissed his forehead and tucked him into bed. Snuggling into his bedclothes, he quickly fell asleep.

How often have you stayed awake all through the night because you were full of fear and anxiety? Just as a loving parent would tell a sleepless, distressed child, "Don't worry. I'm right here, and you don't have to be afraid," God wants you to have faith in Him to banish your fears. *Faith* means to worry not, for confidence will carry you triumphantly through all manner of trials.

Our Father knows that, like little children, we need constant reassurance. Even so, we are sometimes beset by doubts. That is why He says, "The LORD . . . is the One who goes before you. He will be with you, He will not leave you nor forsake you; do not fear" (Deuteronomy 31:8 NKJV). God's Word is true, and the heavenly hand that holds ours and leads us to our destiny is warm and loving.

I was talking to a remarkable woman earlier. She said that

her husband is a longtime diabetic and is now in need of a new kidney. "He goes to dialysis three times a week," she explained. And with tear-filled eyes she uttered, "Thanks be to God, my kidney is compatible to his system, and we are looking forward to a transplant operation. I truly know that prayers work. God has lifted us up many times. I am not afraid of the operation. I know God will be there for us."

So often anxieties stay with us because we don't request God's help. Yes, stress and strain are hard to bear, but the second we call upon God, He is there at our side. Let us ask Him to set us free from anxiety and trust Him to guide us aright.

If you tried to hold a five-pound bag of potatoes for sixty seconds, it might feel a little heavy. But if you held it for an hour, your arm would probably begin to ache. And if you held it nonstop for an entire day, you would definitely be uncomfortable, to say the least! The longer you held it, the heavier it would become.

That is the same way with our worries. If we carry our burdens all the time, soon the burdens become increasingly heavy and too difficult to bear.

Of course, we each can do our part to release ourselves from our burdens. Worry is a useless emotion; it drains our joy and keeps our minds in bondage. When conflicts capture our minds and bind us to mistakes made long ago, we first must learn from those mistakes, then dissolve our attachment to them, leave them in the past, and move ahead to a better day.

It may be helpful to write down your concerns and analyze them one by one. Are they true or imaginary fears? I tried this exercise, and do you know what? After praying and discussing my cares with a trusted confidante, I threw the paper away, knowing my fears were unwarranted. The problem with imaginary worries is that if you allow them to live in you, they can wear you down.

There is a great lesson in the story about the woman who took her problem to the Lord and put it on His altar. Ten minutes later, she was back. She took her problem down again and worried over it. Again she set it on the altar, then came back ten minutes later, took it down again, and worried over it. And yet again, she did the same.

She repeated this same scenario for thirty days. Finally, the woman asked God, "Why haven't You taken care of my worry?" God lovingly replied, "My dear child, if you had just left the problem totally with Me, it would have been solved in three days."

While we should always be striving to improve, we also have to allow God to work in our lives. So let us hand over our problems to God's care, relax, and allow Him to prepare us for the future blessings He has for us. We can affirm His help, grace, and guidance in solving them even before we receive them.

And while we wait for God's grace, we can turn to helping others. In a world of shifting moods, our burdens grow lighter as we help others in need. A kind woman I know once explained to me that whenever she is troubled, she takes bouquets of colorful flowers grown in her garden to people in convalescent homes. By so doing, she forgets her own problems when she sees the happy smiles and glows in the sincere thanks of those people whose lives she touches.

So, when worry keeps you awake through the night, take your burdens to God, finding rest for your soul. As He carries you on angels' wings above your plight, listen as He whispers, "My dear, precious child, go to sleep, and let Me take care of those burdens for you, for I am with you always."

CAST AWAY DOUBTS AND MAKE
ROOM FOR MIRACLES

One day, our curious little daughter Gabriella asked, "Mommy, why can't I see angels?"

Smiling as I remembered asking the same question when I was a child, I replied, "Even though we do not see God, we know He is with us. We can't see love, but we know it's here. It's the same with angels—we have to possess faith that they are all around us."

Our beliefs *do* determine our destiny. In fact, many noble ideas or desires have at first seemed unachievable. But when we look toward triumph, we'll find the courage to continue onward, bringing forth the confidence to do our best.

Recently, a situation occurred in my own life that seemed to foreshadow a potential setback. A business associate called me with adverse news; she believed the launch of one of the products I had created looked grim. I listened carefully to what she was saying, but my heart and mind just couldn't accept her news as the negative she believed it to be.

After she finished talking, I startled her by saying, "That's great!"

There was stunned silence on the other end of the telephone, and then she questioned, "Great? Catherine, did you hear what I just told you?"

"Yes, and this is great news," I confirmed. "God has brought me this far for a reason, and He will not turn His back on me now. Let us thank Him and have faith that this will work out to our advantage. Just wait, and you'll see what I mean."

When I hung up the phone, I expressed gratitude to God,

knowing that He had a good reason for bringing forth this hindrance. Thus I continued to remain faithful, worked hard, and waited expectantly, trusting His perfect timing.

Three months later, we were called to a meeting that proved to be very successful. In fact, we now understood why we had been given a delay; we were far better positioned later to take advantage of new opportunities than we had been before.

Once again, I had seen firsthand that if we have faith and trust and thank God when things seem to rise up against us, He can transform a seeming difficulty into a new occasion to shine; He can turn a closed window into an open door.

Maybe all the odds seem to be against you. Perhaps you have suffered setbacks in the past. And possibly you are full of fear and doubt about the future. Would you believe that success is not determined by having been dealt a good hand? It is determined by taking the hand you were dealt and utilizing it to the best of your ability.

And when you give your total effort, you win regardless of the outcome. The personal satisfaction of trying your best makes you a winner and positively influences those around you.

Who knows what phenomenal things you can achieve for the good of humankind? God is always giving you occasions to move forward, so thank Him and release your faith, knowing that He will constantly be there, right by your side. God uses average people like you and me to do above-average feats.

Now, as I look out the window this evening at the full moon that lights up the landscape, I think to myself, *Everything that has happened in my life, good and bad, has led me to where I am today.*

Life has not always been easy, but whether I was drenched

by the rains of misfortune, stung by the pain of loss, or confronted by countless setbacks, the toughest challenges helped me develop steadfast faith, unwavering persistence, and God-given strength.

And He will do the same for you.

PLANT YOUR SEEDS OF FAITH AND WATCH THEM GROW

Have you ever thought about how the farmers who provide our food live on faith? The farmer, beginning in the chill of the early spring, tills the soil, plants seeds in the ground, fertilizes and waters the crop patiently, then waits day after day, month after month for his harvest.

The farmer has faith in what he cannot see. He has invested thousands of dollars in seeds, plants them in the ground, and knows that they must lie hidden in their tiny shells until they quicken without a ray of sun, splitting apart when their tiny life springs forth. Farmers are the followers of God who, through faith and patience in the long, dark night of waiting, finally inherit the bounty they have awaited.

This year we started a large garden in our backyard. We planted Lauren's favorite vegetable, zucchini, as well as some lettuce, carrots, tomatoes, green beans, red and green peppers, eggplant, and even watermelons.

Todd was faithfully watering the garden early one July evening, and when he reached the eggplant section, he announced, "An animal dug out an entire plant and took it."

Todd continued with his watering.

Late afternoon the next day, Todd examined the eggplant section of the garden again. "Another plant is gone."

Immediately, I thought with a grin, *Well, that is one less eggplant I will have to fry for Eggplant Parmesan!*

But a few days later—you guessed it.

"Catherine," Todd called out, "more plants have disappeared, roots and all!"

So I asked, "What kind of animal do you think is taking the plants?"

"Maybe a raccoon or a skunk. And," he added, "I think the chipmunks are seizing the carrots from under the ground."

"Oh, that's okay, honey," I replied. "Those animals need to eat, too!"

Nevertheless, we faithfully carried on, watering, fertilizing, weeding, and replacing the suspiciously missing plants. And then in early August, overnight it seemed, the watermelons went from the size of golf balls to the size of tennis balls. The zucchini were huge, ready for picking, and we had enough tomatoes to feed everyone on our street. Lauren and Gabriella were happy to gather a basketful of fresh vegetables and take them across the street to our neighbors.

For abundance, we must carry on in faith. Faith changes hopes into actualities. Faith offers an eye that can see the invisible, an ear that hears what others cannot, and a hand that can touch the intangible. There is no limit to the miraculous power of unshakable faith—it can move mountains. When the armor of God and the seed of faith are present in your life, you are like the mighty blade of grass that has the ability to crack open a cement walk.

"What do you do for a living?" a casual acquaintance recently asked me. I thought for a moment and replied, smiling, "I make something from nothing." And then I added, "With faith, God and I create together." I figure, if God created the heavens and the earth, He can certainly help me create beautiful dreams in my life. And I know that He will help to establish wonderful dreams in your life as well.

Faith is a powerful inner assurance that the things we are striving for will take place. It's the knowledge that what we hope for is already ours, even though we have no tangible evidence of this. Our faith is so strong that, despite evidence to the contrary, it cannot be shaken. Faith is an absolute conviction of a truth that has yet to manifest.

Years ago my friend Heather's daughter, Suzie, applied to an outstanding college. It was her first choice, and she had her heart set on going to this excellent school.

Suzie was overjoyed when she received her acceptance letter, but her joy turned to disappointment when she learned the school did not offer any financial aid except the standard government student loan and work study. The tuition, room, and board were more than my friend's entire salary, and as a single parent, she had no other income. But there was another school (although not her first choice) that came forward and offered a full scholarship.

Heather and Suzie attended an open house at the college that was Suzie's first choice. While there, they talked to the financial aid director, who listened to their hopes and dreams. But to their dismay he said, "I think you'd better seriously consider the university that offered you a full scholarship. There is nothing more we can offer you in the way of financial assistance."

Dejected, Heather and Suzie walked out of the room. Then,

for some reason, Heather turned and looked back. "The financial aid director was just staring at us. I felt a kind of tingle, and then the door closed behind us and we went on our way. Suzie took a scheduled tour of the campus, and I went to the chapel. It was so beautiful and peaceful there, I knelt down and prayed for help."

On the way home, Heather suddenly turned to Suzie and said, "Honey, don't worry; you will go to this school. Even if I have to sell our condo and get an apartment, I'll find a way."

They tried to stay positive for the rest of the day and resisted any negative thoughts. Heather had the distinct feeling that God wanted her daughter on that campus.

The very next day, when Heather came home from work, she found a message on her answering machine from Suzie's preferred school. For some reason, the financial aid director had decided to go to his committee and ask if they would help this promising young woman. God's hand was strong, and they agreed to give her a scholarship for the first year. It would be renewed each of the following three years.

Heather and Suzie were ecstatic! They had only to pay room and board, and thanks to government loans and other funding available to parents, Heather was able to pay for the room and board herself.

It doesn't matter what your circumstances look like or how many people tell you what you are trying to do can't be done. Simply persist in your faith, remain optimistic, press on, ask for what you want, and expect the best. And then God will open doors for you.

A reader of my newspaper column from Missouri wrote that

her grandmother taught her the power of faith and how to go to God in prayer. This proved invaluable training, she notes, since we so constantly need God's love and aid.

Scripture says, "Ye have not, because ye ask not" (James 4:2 KJV). Release your faith. Dare to ask. Pray bold prayers, so God can do bold things for you.

A reader told me how he struggled to regain his faith after abandoning it many years before. What kept him going, he said, was a reminder from my column that said, "If I do nothing, there will be nothing for God to bless."

So, returning to the farmer whose livelihood depends on faith, let us follow his example. Let's take that tiny seed and watch as it begins to grow into our dreams.

Remember, the Lord honors those who have not seen yet believe.

BE ENCOURAGED WITH FAITH IN A LOVING GOD

A devoted man of God was tempted by his enemy. How did the evil one plan to do it? Did he plan to show the man the pleasures and excitement of a life of sin? *No, that won't work*, the enemy decided. *The man will know that sin leads to misery.*

Did the enemy show him the trials of a righteous life? *No, that won't work*, the enemy thought, *the man knows that hardships are the paths to wisdom and peace.*

The enemy thought long and hard and then exclaimed, "I will discourage the man's soul and cause him to lose his faith. That will work!"

Take into account that discouragement, doubt, and negativity are our enemies. They are always on the lookout for even the tiniest openings in our minds, where they can insert a toe and work their way in until they have taken control.

Regardless of any discouragement, faith is always courageous. Never faltering, it gives you the courage to persevere and will give you life's greatest reward. Face resistance, walk tall, and just keep on going, even during your toughest moments.

Draw on your incredible resolve to trust God. This alone will build your discipline and determination, helping you view the challenges in your life as opportunities to prove your fortitude. A business colleague once told me, "With God's help, there will always be a rainbow after the storm."

I read in Matthew 9:29, "According to your faith be it unto you" (Matthew 9:29 KJV). Nothing should shake our faith; it is a powerful law that says we will receive either according to our faith or according to our doubt.

We must be obedient to our faith in God's Word. Feelings are variable; they change with the weather. Perfect faith, however, cannot waver. For that reason, I meet doubt with denial and then conquer it with an assertion of faith.

"Therefore, my beloved brethren, be steadfast, immovable, always abounding in the work of the Lord, knowing that your labor is not in vain in the Lord" (1 Corinthians 15:58 NKJV). "The joy of the LORD is your strength" (Nehemiah 8:10 NKJV). The promises of God are so miraculous and incredible. He literally gives us the desires of our hearts.

Now, let me tell you that the enemy failed to tempt the man of God away from his Lord. Do you want to know why? The man's faith was not in himself; it was in a never-failing, always-prevailing, loving, and totally forgiving God. For love never fails.

"How does faith work?" you may ask. Faith works by love. The more we love God, the more faith we will have. Thus, consider the expressions of His love: a baby sweet and precious, the splendor of a majestic tree with its soothing shade, the grandeur of a magnificent sunset, the antics of little animals, the songs of the birds, and the exquisiteness of a flower. All these are expressions of His love for us.

Accordingly, enjoy each precious day, one by one. Awaken to the beauty around you and cherish your every blessing. And know that God gives His best to those who leave the choice with Him.

FAITH: Key to Your Heart's Desire

○──⚷ With faith, every problem can be an opportunity for God to work miracles. Stumbling blocks can be the stepping-stones for your greatest achievements; problems can be turned into glorious possibilities. So look beyond your challenges and put your faith in God.

○──⚷ Regret looks back and anxiety glances around, but faith looks up. Fear ends where faith begins. So close the door of fear behind you and walk through that wonderful open door of faith that is unlocked before you.

○──⚷ In fierce storms, fishermen must do one thing to survive: anchor their ship in a certain position and keep it there. When you are tossed about by afflictions, you must do likewise: place your faith in God, and anchor it there. He is the anchor that holds you steady. In Him, you are immovable and unconquerable.

○──⚷ Weigh all decisions with prayer, seeking God's will and checking out your motivations and objectives. When the answer is not clear, have patience. Sometimes God has a better plan in store and is clearing the way of the other parties concerned.

o—⚷ Whatever happens, have faith in your God-inspired goals. God will complete the good work He began in you and will fulfill the destiny He has arranged.

o—⚷ The essential quality for achievement is never giving up. Continue to press onward with unshakable faith. The last step is usually the winning step.

o—⚷ God does not waste one second of the clock that measures the time of your precious life. Hold an attitude of joyful expectation and faith, and soon you will see your dreams come to pass.

Key #2:
PERSISTENCE

God blesses those who patiently endure testing
and temptation. Afterward they will receive
the crown of life that God has promised to
those who love Him.

(James 1:12 NLT)

I wonder if you have given up on your dreams. Were you told, "No," "It's too late," "You'll never succeed," or simply "Give up!"?

Don't believe the naysayers! Instead, stretch forth your hand, and together we will see how steadfast persistence, determination, and fortitude can open doors. Just remember, it is ultimately up to you to walk through them!

I have found that *persistence* is the word of choice for anyone who seeks success, whether it is in your personal life, home life, or business. I have just one phrase I want you to remember: *It is always too soon to quit!*

As long as you keep on keeping on, that uphill mountain you have been climbing will become the road to a destiny beyond your dreams. Just persist in following it to the best that life has to offer, knowing that faith and persistence are your loyal companions, sent from the One who guides your every step.

PERSISTENCE WILL TRIUMPH OVER
EVERY OBSTACLE

Look up to the heavens, gaze at its numerous stars, and know that your possibilities are as limitless as the universe stretching out before you.

You are endowed with the ability to commune with the eternal. Remember this when you are fighting the feeling of burnout or facing a seemingly unchangeable path.

Just know this: there is no greater awe or unfathomable wonder, delight, or love than beholding God and communing with Him.

Life sometimes gives us challenges, so make decisions with an open heart and determination. You can't just wish for success—a wish changes nothing. But a decision to pray and put your all into the task will change everything.

You might have tried this before and felt that you got nowhere. But the attainment of any prize worth winning demands incredible willpower—day by day, hour by hour, and minute by minute. Opportunities are never lost: someone else will take the ones that you miss, so never quit when you are tired; rather, take another step. The victors always say that it was worth it all. You, too, will see things come out right in time.

I love the story Jesus told about the widow who continued to persevere, even in the face of rejection. Luke 18 tells us about her. This widow had been wronged and wanted justice. The judge finally gave in because the woman was relentless in her pursuit of right action. He said, "I will avenge her [give her what she wants], lest by her continually coming she weary me" (Luke 18:5 KJV).

God loves it when we keep pressing on, persisting when we are tempted to quit, trying again if we don't get as far as we want, then trying again and again. The Bible tells us, "God blesses those who patiently endure testing and temptation. Afterward they will receive the crown of life" (James 1:12 NLT).

In 1999, I received an amazing letter from a naval submarine officer. He was stationed in the Adriatic Sea, and somehow my newspaper column had found its way across the world onto his ship. He said the column inspired him to persevere in pursuit of his goals. No dream is too big, he affirmed, and God would always be available to help him. He quoted Matthew 6:8: "Your Father knows what you need before you ask Him" (Matthew 6:8 NASB).

The column the officer was referring to was a story about a soldier who was forced to hide from his enemies in an abandoned cement silo. The soldier was on the run for days and was exhausted. He was almost at the point of giving up, despairing of rescue.

Lying on the cold, barren floor in the silo, the soldier saw a tiny ant. He looked closer and saw that the insect was carrying a crumb of bread and was attempting to climb up the high, steep wall. The crumb kept falling, but the ant refused to give up.

The soldier counted the ant's efforts to get the crumb up to a window to the outside. Seventy times the crumb fell to the ground. The soldier watched in wonder as the ant patiently shouldered its burden and continued persevering.

On the seventy-first try, the insect reached the top. And that tiny ant's persistence gave the soldier the hope and courage to keep on trying. Two days later, the soldier was able to escape.

Persistence is power. Refusing to give up, especially when faced with opposition, is a sign of strong character. The *Random House Dictionary* defines the verb *persist* this way: "to continue steadfastly, in spite of opposition."

Remember Aesop's race between the tortoise and the hare? The rabbit was arrogant, scoffing at the prospect of racing against a turtle. He took off at breakneck speed and left the turtle spinning in the dust. Then, a mile down the road, he decided to show off by lying down and napping. A deep sleep overcame him, and he slept for hours. But the turtle plugged on and, at his own speed, won the race.

Setbacks can occur from circumstances beyond our control, so if a hurdle arises before you, jump over it or go around it. Be persistent when facing life's challenges, and remember, there's a Higher Power in control. If what you wish is God's will, you will succeed. Thomas Edison made ten thousand tries before coming up with an invention that would light up the world.

If I had a farm with a pond on a hill and I needed to irrigate my garden, I wouldn't just stand by my garden and ask the water in the pond to come moisten my plants. Instead, I would expect to work long, hard hours digging an irrigation ditch and installing pipes so the water would flow to the garden.

It's the same with any goal. Once you have a focus, start the process to make it happen. We all must decide what we'd like to accomplish in life. If we listen to the truth in our hearts and proceed with assurance, we'll find that God is with us, as He is with all faith-filled, persistent people.

I agree with the wisdom of the German philosopher

Goethe: "There are but two roads that lead to an important goal and to the doing of great things: strength and perseverance. Strength is the lot of but a few privileged men, but perseverance may be employed by the smallest of us and rarely fails of its purpose, for its silent power grows irresistibly greater with time."

But best of all are Jesus' words after telling the story of the woman and the judge: "But when I, the Messiah, return, how many will I find who have faith [and are praying]?" (Luke 18:8 TLB).

Will you stand up and be one of them? I believe you will—so stay the course, dear readers, stay the course.

WE CAN ALL LEARN FROM THIS FISH TALE

I heard a cute story about a little fish swimming in the vast blue ocean. The tiny fish was listless and weak as he huddled near the big coral reef.

A large and mighty fish swam past him. Concerned, he asked, "What is the matter, little fish? Is there anything I can do to help you?"

The little fish wearily replied, "I am so tired and thirsty."

"Well," answered the big fish, "start by taking a nice, long drink of water and surely you will feel better and get your strength back."

The little fish quickly answered, "Oh, no, I can't! I just can't!"

"Why?" questioned the big fish.

"I do not want to drink too much water," said the little fish, "because I am afraid it will all run out!"

"Run out!" exclaimed the big fish. "Run out! That's a good

one. This is the Atlantic Ocean! Run out! Ha, ha, ha," laughed the big fish as he swam away.

Sometimes we can behave like the little fish. We settle for lives far below our potential. God has given to us abundantly, and as His children, we are heirs to all.

Therefore, feel free to reach for the highest and the best. God wants you to have success. He delights in your endeavors to please Him. Faith in His generosity can activate your thoughts and actions.

You may be a little fish in the great ocean of life, but everything in that ocean is there for your benefit.

In 1994, when I began working in radio sales, I had no prior selling experience. One of the first events the radio station sponsored was a bridal show. *Well*, I thought, *that is a good place to start*.

So I went through the phone book, made a list of companies that could benefit from radio advertising and a booth in our bridal extravaganza, and telephoned them. First, after introducing myself, I *asked* for an appointment. When they said yes, I took the bridal package, visited the companies, and explained the benefits of being exhibitors in our show. Then I *asked* for the order.

I loved that bridal event and believed in it very strongly. After only two months, I had signed up more than seventy-five new bridal businesses, the most the radio station had ever acquired. I applied that same persistence in *asking* for the order to every account thereafter. In my twelve years in radio sales, each year I always had the most new business. Thus I was the proud recipient of the company's President's Club award many times over.

If you believe in yourself and work hard toward your goals,

you can feel confident to ask for what you want. The greatest step is not wishing for something, but taking action to receive it.

Once I interviewed the CEO of a sportswear company. He told me that he called a national sports league for eight years asking if he could acquire its license. "After phoning thirty-two times in the eight-year period, I finally signed them on," he told me exultantly. "This year, we will do well over $100 million in sales."

We must plan our course of action. At lunchtime, weather permitting, my best friend and I would meet and take thirty-minute walks near our office. I would say to her, "One day, we will work together in our own business." That was fourteen years ago. Today, we do work together for my business, A New You Worldwide.

Do you have a definite goal toward which you can aim? Be extremely focused, precise, and specific about what you want and where you are going.

For Mother's Day one year, Todd bought me a gorgeous watercolor portrait of our home. I like to look at the large, beautiful painting that hangs in our living room and then notice the many little dabs of paint it took to make that picture perfectly complete. It is the same with your plans: just dab a little, bit by bit, until the complete plan has been realized.

Back in the mid-1970s, there was a young boy who loved to play baseball. He was very small for his age and was told early on that he would never be able to play competitive sports because of his size. But the lad, who came from a single-parent home, persisted. He joined community youth leagues and played for every school team he could. In his sophomore year of high school, he tried out for the varsity baseball team and was cut. He was even told by a family member that he could never play baseball.

"You are too small," he was advised. However, the youth did not settle for mediocrity. He persisted and remained positive. He practiced every day, no matter the season, until his hands bled and were covered with calluses. His family room walls and ceiling were filled with dents and holes, as he would practice inside the house in the winter. He lifted weights, exercised, ran with weights, and studied books on baseball.

In his junior year, he tried out again, and that time he made it!

In college, he struggled playing with the varsity team through his freshman and sophomore years, but he stayed with it. He practiced regularly and kept a positive attitude.

And guess what? In his junior year, he won an award as the most improved athlete. And in his senior year, he was named captain of the baseball team, was voted most valuable player, won the college's scholar-athlete award, and was named first-team academic all-American—all this at a Division One college. He persevered and triumphed!

This persistent, determined, fine young man went on to play semipro baseball, then attended Harvard Medical School and today is a doctor at one of America's finest hospitals.

So, like this young man, turn a deaf ear to those who say you are not good enough to achieve your objective. Find out where God wants you to shine and apply perseverance.

I must confess, I'm an all-or-nothing kind of person. If I start a project, I put my whole heart into the endeavor, and I anticipate positive results. Before I begin, however, I always ask myself these three important questions:

1. What is my motive?
2. What is my objective?
3. What is my attitude?

If I can answer from a sincere heart, "To help others and glorify God," then I pray for God's help. Positive determination and a commitment to do good for others will enable you to attain the joy and success you seek.

But always, the key when you pray for success is to ask for God's perfect will for your life. There is no success without God. Seek His will in your life, and you'll find that "no good thing will He withhold from them who walk uprightly" (Psalm 84:11 NKJV).

HE GUIDED MOSES AND HE WILL
LIGHT YOUR WAY

How do we accomplish tasks that are too difficult for us to do alone? Well, we believe, we persevere, and we trust in God to provide the means. If God calls us to it, He will make it possible.

We are told in Exodus that as Moses approached the burning bush, God called to him, "Moses, Moses! . . . Take your sandals off your feet, for the place where you stand is holy ground" (Exodus 3:4–5 NKJV).

The ground was holy because the presence of God was there. And God instructed, "I will send you to Pharaoh that you may bring My people, the children of Israel, out of Egypt" (Exodus 3:10 NKJV).

Moses didn't believe he was capable of doing what God had

asked of him, and he said, "Who am I that I should go to Pharaoh, and that I should bring the children of Israel out of Egypt? . . . O my Lord, I am not eloquent, neither before nor since You have spoken to Your servant; but I am slow of speech and slow of tongue" (Exodus 3:11; 4:10 NKJV).

The Lord responded, "Now therefore, go, and I will be with your mouth and teach you what you shall say" (Exodus 4:12 NKJV). In other words, "I will be with you, Moses," God promised.

Just know this: God's doors are always open to you, regardless of where you come from or what you look like, the obstacles you have faced, or your past mistakes or disappointments. There are no obstacles that can stop you, nor any disadvantage that can hold you back, because God has given you everything you require to succeed. A new chapter in your life can begin today!

There will always be critics and detractors who will try to steer you off course. But here is the key: *what you believe about yourself is what is most important.* Other people do not determine your worth, you do. So take what you have been given and use it to the fullest. Success will be yours, because that's what your Maker wants for you.

Back in her day, Eleanor Roosevelt, the wife of President Franklin D. Roosevelt, was said to be a homely woman who was filled with fear. But one day she made a decision. She took stock of her assets and began to see her true value. She was extremely intelligent, sensitive, and intuitive—and she was wonderful with people! In time, Eleanor Roosevelt became one of the most charming, respected, and influential women in America.

So ignore the skeptics and cynics. The Lord will give you the strength to do what seems impossible. Work diligently toward your goals and pay no attention to doubters and naysayers. As soon as you remove fear, doubt, and worry from your mind, you will free your energy to achieve your heart's desire.

I remember when the son of a friend of mine wanted to apply to an Ivy League college. A well-meaning adult made a big mistake when he warned, "Son, you'll never get into that school. Don't even bother submitting an application." The determined teenager listened respectfully, then decided, *I am going to try anyhow, because I believe this is where the Lord wants me.*

When he let his faith and his heart lead the way, he discovered that the Lord's will was alive within him. He applied to that Ivy League school and was accepted with a scholarship! This year, he is graduating with honors.

Has anyone told you that it is too late to achieve your goals? Grandma Moses, an American folk artist, began her painting career in her seventies and was still painting at one hundred years old.

You say you do not have the finances to make your God-given dream a reality? Mother Angelica, an American nun, founded the Eternal Word Television Network with just two hundred dollars, relying on God's providence. EWTN now reaches more than a hundred million viewers in hundreds of countries around the world.

Do you feel you have physical limitations? Beethoven, who was deaf, continued to compose masterpieces, conducting and performing, for he heard within himself some of the greatest music the world has ever known.

Even if you can't stand up or walk, you can still be president of the United States. Franklin D. Roosevelt, our thirty-second president, was paralyzed by polio and lost the use of his legs, but he had such a determined spirit that he reduced his handicap to an inconvenience in his own mind.

Have you gone through a devastating experience? Nelson Mandela emerged from twenty-seven years of imprisonment, and to everyone's surprise, his outstanding compassion and humanity shone as brightly as when he went in. He had endured adversity with a sense of purpose and determination to survive and share his strength with others.

Perhaps someone told you that you could not accomplish a goal. Now, take a look at Helen Keller, whose devoted teacher, Anne Sullivan, helped her to believe she could learn to communicate, even though a childhood illness had left Helen deaf and blind. Helen went beyond simply learning to communicate and graduated from college with honors. She then devoted her life to helping others, becoming an articulate writer for the dignity of all individuals. She wrote, "Self-pity is our worst enemy and if we yield to it, we can never do anything wise in this world."

Helen Keller's sterling example gives hope to millions of people who are tempted to give up. She felt God's guidance with her at all times and followed its light to deep personal fulfillment, despite her handicaps.

These are only a few of the many examples of those who totally transcended adversity through perseverance and overcame their challenges.

Therefore, if you ask yourself, as Moses did, *Who am I?* allow me to remind you: *You are a child of God. Your value is beyond measure. You are capable and significant. You deserve the best. God delights in you.* And today, someone is waiting for and needs to receive a sign of self-worth from you.

Remember, God's love extends far beyond any human love. Accept Him as your life partner, and let Him lead the way.

ADVERSITY CAN LEAD US TO ADVANTAGE

Often I have found that our setbacks can blaze the way to future successes.

An old legend tells of the time a powerful hurricane swept through the forest. The great wind took all the beautiful leaves off a picturesque, grand oak tree. It snapped the tree's boughs, broke each branch in two, shook its limbs, and pulled its bark until the oak tree was stark and weak.

Nevertheless, the oak held its ground.

Surprised, the wild wind spoke, "How can you still be standing, Mr. Oak?"

The oak calmly replied, "I have deep roots that are stretched into the good earth. You will never touch them. For you see, Mr. Wind, today I have found out just how much I can endure, and thanks to you, I am stronger than I ever knew."

The storms we experience certainly will not cease, but by the grace of God we can choose to persevere, become stronger, rise above, and learn from them.

Perhaps the greatest test of courage is to endure defeat without losing heart. We need the courage to pursue our convictions, the courage to wait patiently in faith, and the courage to see things through. Then, all at once, we'll be given an opportunity that can make all the difference.

I have kept a journal for the past few years of the losses, setbacks, complications, rejections, unfair occurrences, and unforeseen struggles I have encountered. Recently, I looked at the two long pages I had written down in a notebook detailing my trials and the circumstances that I tried to overcome.

What I found most remarkable was that shortly after the adverse circumstance—sometimes within days—I would be given a taste of victory. Accomplishing my goal would arrive just before the point at which defeat almost overtook me. And if I did not know where to turn, out of the blue a new idea would take me in a whole new direction.

Now when I go through a situation I do not comprehend, I tell the Lord, "You give me the strength, dear Lord, and I will carry on," then I tell myself: *This challenge is an opportunity for me to think bigger. The future is promising, and God is working this together for good. Praise Him.* I might not be able to see how things will transpire, but I know God has a solution.

"Do you ever wonder why these things happen?" you might inquire. Sure. But I declare with assurance, "Lord, I know You are with me, and though I can't understand *why* some things happen, I trust in You and I will do my part by persevering."

And when conditions are too difficult for me to endure alone, I affirm, "I release this to You, Lord. I know You will work this out for Your glory and my good." Then, with resolve, I carry on.

To the gardener, the purpose of *pruning* is clearly understood. Cutting back, if done at the right time, can generate a marvelous transformation and cause the plants to produce in abundance.

Our lives can be like the plants and trees growing in the garden—at times pruning may be necessary. And even though the pruning might be painful, these cutbacks have a gracious purpose. In the process of growth, it is essential for pruning to be done on the branches that will bear fruit so they can bring forth *more* fruit.

Therefore, if something did not happen the way you had hoped it would, know that just up ahead, God has another branch that is waiting to blossom and a greater design for your life.

Recently I received a remarkable letter from a dear reader. She explained how she was just sixteen years old when she had her first child, and by the time she was twenty-three she had five children. Her dream was to go to medical school, but because of her situation she was not able to finish high school. Instead, she got her GED.

Through the years, she kept her dream alive to go into the medical profession. She prayed for God to help and guide her to where she could best serve His purpose. Her first real attempt at college came after two failed marriages. And with sole responsibility for the children, she took a leap of faith and enrolled in school.

The day before her first day of college, she had an electrical fire at the home in which she and her children lived, and they had to move out and remained homeless for five months. Still, she persevered with her dream.

In those five months, this amazing woman kept going to school and never missed a day. She wrote that in her first semester she had to take a class called Investment in Success. It was full of positive thinking and encouraging affirmations, and it was like a magnifying glass that looked deep into her soul. She believed that God and the lessons in that class saved her from a life of destruction.

For the next sixteen months of her new education, she thought positively, created more and more affirmations, and kept soul-searching, even throughout what appeared to be the worst of times.

This inspiring woman graduated with a degree in respiratory care and was honored as student of the year. She had perfect attendance and held a 3.7 grade point average, which put her at the top of her class. She eventually donned the cap and gown and strode across a stage to receive her diploma. Today her children are thriving, and she is pursuing a career in her chosen field. All the previous hardship ended in pure triumph.

I believe that when we pray for strength, God may respond by giving us difficulties to make us stronger. If we ask for wisdom, He may then give us problems to solve. When we request prosperity, God gives us the fortitude to work hard. As we need courage, He grants the challenges to overcome. And when we ask for His support, God gives us opportunities.

I asked for love and God supplied me with people I could help. Through Him, I receive everything I need. I feel so secure in His hands. His magnificent grace and presence are with me—as they are with you—in every circumstance.

God transforms setbacks into victory as you look upward to the great Creator of the universe. He can transform an affliction into an affirmation, for I know the Bible says, "Commit your works to the LORD and your plans will be established" (Proverbs 16:3 NASB).

PUT ONE FOOT IN FRONT OF THE OTHER AND REACH YOUR GOALS

I see him walking every morning. Bit by bit, one step after another, wearing a baseball cap and red fleece jacket, he inches his way down the winding road. This man resides just outside my neighborhood, and when he sees me approaching, pushing Sophia in the stroller, he lifts his head from his apparent concentration and gives me a wave and a warm smile.

In the heat of the summer or the cold blast of winter, he walks. Small steps. Unhurriedly. Slowly, but surely.

Sometimes he staggers just a few feet, but other days he walks a half block and occasionally a mile, I am told. But always, he persists. If he stumbles or trips, he gets back up, brushes himself off, and tries again.

Frequently, he is with a nurse, now and then with a friend, and other times he walks alone.

I don't know this gentleman personally, but I admire his courage, his fortitude, his determination . . . and even in the midst of struggle . . . his joy.

This takes me back to a young couple who had a dream of owning their own home. They couldn't afford, at that time, to buy a house, but they did manage to save up enough money for a small down payment on some land.

Once they had the lot, they drew up some rough plans and sketches on paper. Weekly, they went to their land with a tape measure, string, and stakes and made an outline of their dream house. This went on month after month, year after year.

The couple persevered and took on extra jobs to save enough earnings to put into their house fund. After ten years, the couple took their plans and their savings to a mortgage company, hired a contractor, and built their dream house.

"Catherine, isn't it difficult to continue when the going is slow?" you may ask. Yes, most certainly. But I'd like to remind you that maximum success in life is found by taking one small step at a time. A building is built with one brick at a time, right? And, every great accomplishment is a series of little steps.

There are no shortcuts to achieving something extraordinary. Time, dedication, and effort go into a quality life. The

winners are those who work hard, walk bravely, and climb the mountain—even if it is steep and rough.

An eloquent example of unwavering conviction is found in Matthew 15:21–28. These Scripture verses tell the story of a woman who had great faith. And because of the woman's perseverance, Jesus healed her daughter's body miraculously.

Jesus was in the Canaanite land to find quietness and rest. We read in Matthew 15 that a woman of Canaan cried to Jesus: "Have mercy on me, O Lord, Son of David! My daughter is severely demon-possessed" (Matthew 15:22 NKJV).

But the next verse says that the Lord did not answer her. He remained quiet.

What would you do if you asked someone a question and your request was ignored? Would you give up because of hurt feelings?

The Canaanite woman persisted and did not yield to Jesus' silence. Her afflicted daughter was in need of healing, and she knew that Jesus could supply that need.

Then the disciples said, "Send her away, for she cries out after us" (Matthew 15:23 NKJV).

If this happened to you, would you then just retreat?

The Canaanite woman stayed firm, not letting even the disciples stand in her way.

So Jesus answered, "I was not sent except to the lost sheep of the house of Israel" (Matthew 15:24 NKJV)—meaning that He was not there for her.

But she did not let that obstacle stop her. Instead, she carried on, worshiping and praising Jesus, no matter the circumstance. "Lord, help me!" she uttered (Matthew 15:25 NKJV).

Jesus replied, "It is not good to take the children's bread and throw it to the little dogs" (Matthew 15:26 NKJV).

Determined, this woman again did not concede and turn away. Instead she persistently yet humbly pleaded, "Yes, Lord, yet even the little dogs eat the crumbs which fall from their masters' table" (Matthew 15:27 NKJV).

Jesus then gave her the mercy that she sought, saying unto her, "O woman, great is your faith! Let it be to you as you desire" (Matthew 15:28 NKJV). And her daughter was made whole from that very hour.

The Canaanite woman was tried and tested, and her reaction to these tests determined her and her daughter's destiny.

God looks for that same kind of strong conviction and fortitude in all of us.

Early on, when we first started our business, I remember calling my minister seeking advice. "I am having setback after setback in the development of my inspirational product line. Sales outlets for the products are uncertain, and I am having a difficult time with a person I am doing business with . . . among countless other things.

"Pastor," I said, "maybe this was not a good idea after all and I should return to my radio career."

The minister listened to my dilemma and told me a memorable story that I will never forget. He said he was driving on an unfamiliar road when he began to get lost and kept thinking that he should turn back. This went on for quite a while. It started to get dark outside, and he grew afraid that he was going to become disoriented. Well, he decided keep going forward, and just a few miles up the road he found his way back on track. He had been closer to his destination than he had thought.

The moral of the narrative is that many times we do not know how close we are to something special when we get fearful and turn back, missing what God has in store for us. If we give up, we will never know how close we were to success. It might be just around the next curve in the road.

The key? It's when times get the toughest that you must not quit. It requires stamina to be victorious, so stick to your goals until they come to completion. You never can tell how close you are to your objective. In a *moment* you can be blessed in a manner that you never thought possible.

Four months after that conversation with my minister, I launched eleven new inspirational products successfully on television, with nine of them becoming instant sellouts! A national magazine phoned and wrote a story about my product line, helping with Web site sales. Then, after receiving a letter from a gentleman in Australia who loved my dinnerware, I got the idea to license Grace Line for worldwide distribution.

The catchphrase of life must be *Never give up*. Keep on trying, and eventually you will achieve. I'm partial to this quote from American author Harriet Beecher Stowe: "When you get into a tight place and everything goes against you, till it seems as though you could not hold on a minute longer, never, ever give up, for that is just the place and time that the tide will turn."

Therefore, with gladness, hour by hour and day by day, keep on striving, press onward, and move forward. With every step, God is saying to you today, "*I will be with you.*"

PERSISTENCE:

Key to Your Heart's Desire

○━ In life, we get only those things for which we search, dig, and strive. God-inspired dreams are powerful, but they come true only when backed up by action. So dare to ask for what you want, forget the "what-ifs," and reach for what you thought was an unreachable star.

○━ We all encounter difficulties, but as we continue to move forward, we discover that these very obstacles shape our character. Be persistent when confronting life's challenges. View obstacles as learning experiences, for success is measured by the obstacles one has conquered.

○━ Be patient. Success is a continuous journey—it takes time. Pray continually for God's leading, continue striving, never yield, and ultimately you will achieve according to God's design.

○━ Remember, an ant moves a hill one grain of dirt at a time. In the end, the ant moves the entire

mountain. Take the next step. You don't have to climb the whole staircase now, just take the first step to attain your heart's desire.

o—➤ Each of us is endowed with a gift. Therefore, take the exceptional gift God has given to you and make the very most of it. It is not too late to discover all the wonder you can achieve and offer it to others in the form of service, blessing humankind.

o—➤ Believe in your own worth, and with a humble yet reasonable confidence, develop a healthy self-respect. Walk with your head held high and remember you are a child of an all-powerful, all-loving God. And with His strength, you can conquer anything that tries to come up against you.

o—➤ Just try taking a slipper away from a puppy that has a good grip on it. You can lift the puppy right up in the air, but he won't let go. . . . Get that kind of hold on your dreams, and you will be lifted right up into the winner's circle where you belong!

Key #3:
OPTIMISM

Whatsoever things are true, whatsoever things
are honest, whatsoever things are just, whatsoever
things are pure, whatsoever things are lovely,
whatsoever things are of good report;
if there be any virtue, and if there be any praise,
think on these things.

(Philippians 4:8 KJV)

I have decided to be optimistic, every single day, each moment, with every breath I take. Optimism is a choice. We create our happiness thought by thought, action by action, deed by deed.

Join me on this journey, dear reader. Together we will turn the joy-filled corner and enter a new path full of new opportunities, greater blessings, renewed health, and total victory. This is a time of endless possibilities, grand discoveries, and richer experiences than we have ever imagined.

No matter who you are, regardless of what you have been through, with optimism you can transform life's temporary obstacles into gifts. This is a new day—and it's your day. As you begin this most important passage in your life, I ask only that you focus on this thought: God has placed along your path opportunities for great achievement. He has called you by name and made you in His own image to accomplish incredible things.

Now, with an optimistic mind-set, let's reach as high as we can and touch the fabric of our true potential.

Are you ready to start?

"BE OF GOOD CHEER" 365 DAYS A YEAR

When I see my middle daughter smile, the sweet dimple in her cheek so prominent, I am reminded of my mother, who had the same eye-catching dimple. But more important, I recall my mother's remarkable good nature, which is also apparent in my small, darling daughter.

An inexhaustible good nature is one of the most precious gifts from God. It spreads itself like liquid sunshine and keeps the mind equable in the toughest times. I know the Bible says to "be of good cheer." This statement was not just frivolously thrown out to us, for the phrase that followed it held the key: "Be of good cheer, I have overcome the world" (John 16:33 NKJV)—the entire world in all its turbulent ways.

Therefore, if we believe God to be in us, we know we have the wisdom and power that will overcome every situation. So "be of good cheer," for He has also said, "I will never leave you nor forsake you" (Hebrews 13:5 NKJV). If God said it to be so—then I believe.

Let us consider how we can spend our days in "good cheer." Every morning is a bright invitation to make our lives more meaningful and more precious than the day before. Morning is the awakening hour, the best time of the day to elevate our lives by saying "Good morning" to God, for He has been protecting us as we slept through the night.

With the dawn comes the awareness that we have been granted another opportunity to sing His praises, just as the birds in the trees sing their songs of welcome to each new day.

And how are Todd and I greeted every morning? We hear the sweet song of our three daughters, who turn their faces up to ours and greet us with a loving "Good morning, Mama. Good morning, Daddy," excited to welcome the day that will unfold before them.

Here is the key: if you so desire, you can begin each morning with that very same sense of joy. Whatever you do in word or deed, do it as unto the Lord. You, too, can decide to awaken with a song of praise in your heart to our heavenly Father, making this a part of your life as easily as my small daughters do.

Simplicity brings forth the highest life. To be content with little is a virtue of the wise. Love, peace, health, and joy are a few of the results of praise. Renewing ourselves each day can refresh our hearts, even as we listen to the still, sweet voice within.

At the beginning of the year, I bought each of my two oldest daughters a calendar to hang in their rooms. On this particular calendar, under the date there is a place to write a little something for the day. What amazes me is that each and every day, seven-year-old Gabriella writes, "Good day!" at the close of the evening.

Certainly, at such a young age, she has captured the joy of life and makes the choice to be happy, regardless of circumstances. And we can do the same.

There is a proverb that says, "Happiness is the result of making a bouquet of those flowers within reach." Every day is important. At every moment, humanity makes decisions that determine its eternal destiny. With a little more deliberation about our choice of pursuits, we can turn the corner and behold a whole new world.

Each morning I pray for God's grace and for His peace, and

surely He gives it to me. For happy are those who are wise enough to seek contentment by close companionship with the Lord. He always lifts me from my lows, gives me remarkable strength, and restores me while I sleep, so I will awaken renewed and invigorated.

Being good-natured positively affects those around us. It spreads joy, hope, and real love, while creating ever-spreading ripples of the wonders of life. We can focus on just making a living . . . or we can design a full, joyful, and contented existence.

Let us greet every morning with joy and every evening with peace. Each day is a precious gift from God, so let us seek contentment as we begin the day with praise and end it with prayer.

Simply begin, "Father God, thank You for all the angels around us." For me, the angels take the form of my three delightful, darling daughters. Now, ask yourself, *Who are* my *angels?*

A MOTHER'S OPTIMISM IS A FAMILY LEGACY

Sometimes for a moment, and usually longer, I stand in front of my mother's framed photograph on the desk in my office. When I gaze at it, it brings to mind one of my most comforting childhood memories. . . .

When I was a little girl, I would sit in an old rocking chair with my mother as she told me stories. Mother didn't use the language or narratives of a philosopher, but in her own sweet words, she took the time to explain to me the importance of the simple things of life.

Because of her positive attitude toward life, she could transform an ordinary day into an extraordinary delight. Her remarkable good nature and sunny disposition radiated to everyone she met, and she was a living testament to the word *optimism*.

The Random House Dictionary defines optimism as "the tendency to look on the more favorable side of happenings, the belief that good ultimately predominates over evil."

I believe one of the secrets of my mother's optimistic attitude was her warm, loving upbringing. Mother was raised by wonderful parents. "My parents did everything together," she recalled, her face glowing as she spoke, "and my father even came shopping with us to buy me shoes. He was such a good, honest man." To this day, I recall this story when Todd and I go shopping together to buy shoes for our three daughters.

Back in the early 1920s, my grandfather worked two jobs to support his wife and six daughters. My grandmother helped everyone. Whatever someone needed, she would provide joyfully, whether it was cooking, baking, babysitting, or cleaning. By her example, she went on to instill that quality of joy and helpfulness into her children.

Through the stories my mother told me about her own parents, I began to learn what qualities to look for in a husband. "Don't judge someone on their outward appearance," she would say. "Go for a person's character."

From my mother, I learned how to create a happy home. "We never had any money when I was a young girl," she would reminisce, "but our home was filled with laughter, joy, and peace."

The attitude that dwells in a home can make it wonderful or difficult, can inspire or defeat. A loving atmosphere is the foundation for our lives and our families' futures. Therefore, we must strive to create peace and gentleness in all our ways with our spouses and children.

I like this saying: "The beauty of the house is order, the blessing of the house is contentment, the glory of the house is hospitality." Praising God, being thankful, and having things in order can create a sanctuary for our families and enhance the joy in our lives.

Mother taught me about sharing, being thoughtful, and remembering birthdays and other special occasions. "Let's walk to the corner store to purchase a greeting card," she'd suggest, and then hand in hand we would.

If people visited, she would snip a piece of ivy off her houseplant and give it to them to take home so they could enjoy its beauty, too. Mother loved to crochet, and she merrily made blankets, tablecloths, and sweaters. She believed the generous giving of ourselves produces the generous harvest.

My mother taught me to work hard, too. Whether she was carefully ironing our freshly laundered clothes, meticulously pin-curling my long hair, or working at a local clothing store, she suggested, "You must always put love into what you do."

Our greatest lessons can often be painful. I recall coming home from grade school upset because I had been teased by some of the girls. Then Mother would play a game with me or we'd sing some songs. By the time we finished, I wasn't sad anymore. "Don't worry," she'd say. "God has a way of turning things around."

And I learned not to be preoccupied with seeking approval from others. "Follow your heart," Mother would say. "Just be yourself."

Sometimes she'd caution, "Be careful who you trust. No matter how pleasant some people appear to be, give your heart with caution." I know the Bible says to "beware of false prophets, who come to you in sheep's clothing, but inwardly they are ravenous wolves" (Matthew 7:15 NKJV); and "He who walks with wise men will be wise" (Proverbs 13:20 NKJV). In other words, we must choose our friends wisely and observe who has earned our trust as well as who has not.

I discovered early on that life is short, so we mustn't waste a moment on feeling discouraged, negative, or regretful. For the time we are allotted, we must choose to be optimistic and to spin from life all the love, goodwill, and courage we can in order to pursue our God-given dreams.

In the case of setbacks, I remember my mother saying, "Everything happens for a reason. You may not see it now, but you will eventually."

My mother's strong faith helped me, even as a child, understand God. She presented faith as a normal part of our lives. As a result, I opened to it very easily and naturally, following her example. When we bring up our children with God's wisdom to guide them, they can walk through the difficulties of the world with optimism and faith, secure that He will protect them.

The Bible reminds us, "The memory of the righteous is blessed" (Proverbs 10:7 NKJV). Life may not always have been easy for me, but it was a blessed life because I had a praying mother, and she lived a life that honored God. I can still hear her tenderly say, "Pray, Catherine, and God will help us." Those words still guide me beyond any temporary darkness into the bright rays of sunlight.

Many, many years have passed since those days when I sat contentedly with my mother. Yet her memory strikes a vibrant chord as I sit with my own sweet daughters and tell them stories about my optimistic mother, hearing the echo of Mom's voice within my own.

Over the mists of time I hear: "I just want you to be happy." "Be yourself." "Always be nice to everyone." "I am proud of you." "Always do right." "I love you."

Or is it my voice that I hear, speaking these very words to my children? As I share with my daughters the things that my mother told me, I know I am handing over love's legacy.

Today, when I linger in the office in front of my mother's photograph, I wish she were here to see how joyful I am as I follow her advice. Then, in less than an instant, I somehow feel that she is smiling down at us over the banister of heaven. And knows.

DEVOTE YOUR TIME TO A CAUSE
THAT SERVES GOD

Time is a precious gift: we must navigate our lives guarding it as a cherished possession and spending it wisely.

For me, the value of guarding time is more apparent now that I live outside the city. There is nothing more glorious than being inspired by the gorgeous lilac color of the early morning sky, the sound of geese flying overhead, and the peaceful comforts of home.

"Mommy, look! The clouds are so puffy, it looks like God is coming out of them!" my perceptive daughter Gabriella shouted delightedly when she was only four, her tiny finger pointing up to the heavens.

Like my daughter, I love to observe nature's beauty. As I sip my morning coffee, I delight in the harmony of the universe. Nature brings us healing in heart, soul, and mind, and as I observe His perfect creation, I thank God for making me aware of His love for us.

I realize that here, outside the hubbub of the city, I am changing. I am reshaping my thinking about how I will spend my time, acutely aware of how I use my moments, my hours. Robert Louis Stevenson wrote, "To change one's mind under changed circumstances is true wisdom."

Now that we live in the country on two glorious wooded acres, I find that creating balance in my life is crucial. I have learned to simplify my days, to take time to putter in the garden, to feed the birds, to enjoy a walk along the countryside, and to be alone with my own thoughts. Everything turns out better when I take time for renewal, resting my mind and refreshing my spirit.

We all know how to rush and hurry, but tranquility is essential to our well-being. Let's be sure to include it in our lives!

Once I was asked, "Catherine, how can we hold on to time, our most valued commodity, making the most of it and not wasting a second?"

An answer, I think, lies in the words of a dear friend who said, "Time is relative to our obedience to God. He can stretch it out when we obey His will."

I believe the value of time isn't in how many years we have on earth, but what we do with our years. And by putting God first in our lives and walking with Him according to His plan, we are living lives full of purpose. God can take one second and turn it into an eternity.

Take just five minutes to ask God to expand your hours. As you go about your day, if a worry or problem arises, stop for a moment and ask, "Father, is this the right thing to do? If not, please show me the way." Then, leave the issue in His hands. Hour by hour you will feel relieved, loved, and protected.

Worry is a thief of our precious time; it robs us of our lives—past, present, and future. Know that if you continually worry about a situation, you are stifling the creative ability within you that can solve the problem. Therefore, when you take a positive outlook and expect the best, the problem can reverse itself and become a blessing in disguise.

Sheila, an editor friend, told me about a recent experience with a publisher. She had rushed to get him a proposal for an important meeting in which the decision makers would discuss whether or not a book would be right for them. When she spoke to the sponsoring editor the morning of the meeting, he told her, "I'm so sorry, but one of our staff members can't make the meeting, so it's been postponed."

Immediately, she said, "Well, I guess a Higher Power set this up, so there must be a reason for the delay we don't know about." The editor laughed, but Sheila was right. As they continued discussing the book idea, she realized there were a few key points missing in the proposal. She now had some time to gather the missing information, which would strengthen its chances of acceptance. The following week, the publisher happily announced that the company would be buying the book.

Experiences like Sheila's show us that we have to permit God time to work in our lives and look ahead with a positive attitude. Let's relax and affirm and confirm His help, grace, and guidance even before we request them. Say, "Thank You, Lord, for the blessings that I know are even now on their way to me."

Accordingly, let us make the most of our precious time, nur-

turing our souls by creating a quiet place to read, pray, or medi-
tate. There is an abundance of ways through which we can transform ourselves. This is our chance to regroup, unwind, and gain
strength. We need to take time to replenish the force that holds
us up so we can move forward and follow God's lead.

We know we must feed ourselves every day or our bodies
will become sickly and weak. So must we feed our spirits and
souls and give ourselves occasions to just do nothing. Communing with nature, taking an afternoon nap, browsing at tag sales,
taking a drive in the country, and enjoying a cup of tea with a
neighbor can revitalize and rejuvenate us.

Are you an avid gardener? Do you love to paint, sing, or
write? Take the time to enjoy a favorite activity.

My friend Laura always wanted to learn to ice-skate profes-
sionally. Now, in her forties, she has a coach, skates five mornings
a week, is going to skating camp, and even plans to compete. "I
just love it!" she exclaims.

I also know someone who delights in her garden and who put
in a little goldfish pond amid beautiful wildflowers. She has created a meditation place to calm her spirit. She practices breath-
ing deeply to soothe every nerve in her body, and as she sits on
a comfortable lounge chair, she closes her eyes and listens to the
murmur of the wind.

Lately, I've been taking one step at a time instead of running
at full speed. I notice that when I don't unwind after nonstop
activity, my outlook can become weary.

Therefore, I must uplift my spirit in the midst of silence,
through prayer and a devotional search for God's promises. I set
aside time to tune into calmness, to tranquility, to listen to the
birds and feel the gentle breeze.

I hear the tiny frogs and crickets sing me to sleep at night, and though I like to sleep at bedtime, I just can't wait until morning. Awakening early, as darkness slowly vanishes through the dawning light, I catch a glimpse of God. He is present in every sunrise, in the blades of dewy grass, and in each loving thought.

Optimistically, I ponder the inspiration that God puts in my heart. *Something incredibly wonderful is always within reach*, I remind myself as I savor the beginning of a new day. I know that we are here on this earth to know Him, to thank Him, to fill each day with His delightful will, and to enjoy this wonderful time He has given us.

REMEMBER TO TRUST IN GOD

One day I had lunch with a friend at a lovely shoreline restaurant. Our conversation turned to a column that I had written years earlier about the importance of thinking positive.

In that column, I told a story about an old Indian chief and a young preacher. The two men were talking, and the Indian chief admitted, "Ever since I have given my heart to God, dear preacher, I find that within me there is a fight between the black dog and the white dog."

Listening carefully, the preacher questioned, "Chief, tell me, which one wins?"

The wise old Indian chief remained silent for a few minutes, then gave an insightful answer: "The one I feed the most."

My friend and I agreed how crucial it is to feed our minds continually with good, constructive thoughts, for the mind, like the body, needs nourishment.

"And if we do this," I said, "over a period of time, we can condition our minds to automatically react optimistically to any adverse situations we encounter. We can train our thoughts on whatever things are pure, whatever things are just, whatever things are lovely and of a good report, cherishing the gift of life, embracing it, and making the most of it. Our thoughts can determine what we have or what we will become."

At that precise moment, a lady approached our table. Leaning toward me, she said, "I want you to know how much I enjoy your weekly column, Catherine."

I replied, "Oh, thank you!"

The lady then said, "I want you to know I loved the column you wrote about the black dog and the white dog."

My friend and I looked at each other in amazement, nodding our heads at the astonishing coincidence. "We were just talking about that same article!" he declared enthusiastically.

What you have said or done today may affect what you will be next week. The thoughts that will be the strongest tomorrow are those you have fed today. If you want to know what will likely be in your future, notice your dominant thought pattern. Whatever types of thoughts you have most often can activate forces to produce conditions that will match your expectations and thus create your future.

What thoughts play in your mind again and again? It is universally known that what you think, you will become, and your thoughts are the foundation of your character, your happiness, and your successes or failures.

Never let any negative emotions run away with you. Take as much care with what goes into your mind as with what food you put in your mouth. If there was any question that certain foods were tainted, you wouldn't touch them, would you?

What do you watch on television or view on the Internet? Do the words of your favorite songs promote violence or peace? How about your friends—do you associate with loving people who have optimistic mind-sets?

Be watchful; attitudes are transferable, and within a short time a pessimistic person can drain you of your most wonderful aspirations. You must tune out the naysayers and refuse to let cynics weigh you down. The actions of someone who says or does something hurtful reflect on himself or herself, not you.

Choose to move away from these people and concentrate on the constructive and positive. Keep cheerful, honest friends near you who are heartening and helpful. Seek out joy-filled, encouraging individuals. When you need them, they'll be there.

I love the two requirements that Mother Teresa had for those working with her in Calcutta: a desire to work and a joyful attitude. And I earnestly agree! A positive attitude is of the utmost importance. In fact, one of the main reasons I chose to work with the Hachette Group to publish this new book was because of the staff's tremendous optimism and positive energy!

A gentleman I used to work with in the radio business often told us, "Always think and be positive. . . . Life is too short not to." We need to remember that our destination is not really a place, but rather the attitude with which we approach our lives.

Try behaving as if you were brimming with esteem and overflowing with optimism. When you take your eyes off the positive, even for a moment, you can begin spiraling downward. So cast out negative ideas and believe the best! Visualize victory and turn your mind toward things that are pleasant and affirmative.

About eight months ago, I spoke to a young woman who had been diagnosed with a rare disease. Instead of being depressed, she optimistically spoke about how blessed she had been, and how grateful she was to God. This woman had many reasons to be negative and bitter, but she chose to see her circumstances differently, and with steadfast efforts and positive affirmations she refocused her beliefs.

When I asked for her secret, she told me, "I use my mind to focus on that which is good, not on the conditions around me that I cannot immediately change. And I pray daily and have faith in a loving God who sustains me."

Expressing our heartfelt thoughts to God and listening to His response brings us wisdom, peace, and contentment. As we lean on Him, our worries and heartaches cease, and we can gain the wisdom, strength, and courage to carry on. Our cares and woes come into perspective, and His love for us becomes the greater object of our thoughts.

I have found that in times of trouble, we must especially guard our thoughts, for it is especially then that harmful, negative thoughts can bombard us.

In the Bible, it says that when the apostle Paul looked at the Roman soldier assigned to guard him, he was reminded that our battle is a spiritual fight. This Scripture prompts us to "put on the full armor of God" so that we might stand firm in the struggles of life (Ephesians 6:11 NIV).

According to *The American Heritage Dictionary*, *armor* is defined as "a defensive covering worn to protect the body against weapons." So with prayers and faith, put on that armor, for you, too, are called to be a spiritual soldier and fight the good fight of faith, confident that God has equipped you well for your journey.

In the book of Ephesians I found the Scripture that also tells us about "the helmet" (Ephesians 6:17 NIV). A most critical part of our armor, a helmet is a covering that protects the head. Moreover, this image reminds me that our way of thinking needs safeguarding, because our mental attitude is vital when we need to make correct moral and spiritual decisions.

Therefore, rather than becoming submissive and letting just any thought linger, rise up and be strong, filling your mind with an overflowing of faith, love, and optimism, so there will be no room for doubt or discouragement.

You were created to excel, to achieve your goals, and to successfully bring about what God has called you here to accomplish. To make room for all the good things you want to transpire in your life, create and nourish them first in your thoughts. Once they have begun to take root and grow, you can move forward and start to transform your world.

THE JOY YOU SHARE WILL RETURN TENFOLD

Life is reciprocal. The genuine kindness, goodness, and helpfulness you expend will always come back to you. Divine abundance follows the laws of service and generosity. By lifting up others, you lift up yourself, for God knows our truest happiness is found in serving Him and loving others. From such loving acts, a love of life and an optimistic heart will begin to blossom.

There's a little verse I like that says, "From what we get, we can make a living; but what we give to others makes life worth living."

Years ago, a friend's husband was in the hospital the day they

were to celebrate fifty years of marriage. Without anyone knowing, I went to the florist and bought a dozen long-stemmed red
roses and a card. In simple printing I wrote, "I love you. Happy
50-year Anniversary." I left the card unsigned, printed my friend's
name on the envelope, inserted the card, and attached it to the
floral arrangement.

Then I went to my friend's apartment building and left the
fragrant bouquet inside the front foyer of the complex. I figured
someone would see the flowers and take them to her. Chuckling,
I thought that if someone saw me, they would think I was the
floral delivery person.

A few hours later my friend phoned me. "Catherine," she
said between tears, "my husband had flowers sent to me for our
anniversary!"

"That's wonderful!" I told her, happy to share her joy. I never
told anyone that story until now, for it comforts me to know
that I was able to do a kind deed for that sweet woman. That
day turned out to be one of the last times I spoke to her. Shortly
thereafter, her husband passed away, and soon after, she did as
well.

If we make it our goal to live lives of caring, compassion, and
unconditional love, the world then becomes an opportunity to
create joy. A cherished friend reminded me of a saying: "I went
outside to find a friend and could not find one there. I went outside to be a friend and friends were everywhere." Let us bring
our own individual sunshine wherever we go.

With a smile, stop for a moment and hold the door open for
the person behind you. And do more than take bouquets of flowers to patients in a hospital. Sit down, take their hands, and say a
prayer with them for a quick recovery.

I'm acquainted with a kind woman named Vivian who takes her sweet-natured French poodle on visits to the local nursing home. How happy she makes the residents as they pet and cuddle her endearing four-pound dog.

Vincent, a longtime friend, drives an older neighbor to her doctor's appointment every week and then takes her out to lunch.

A benevolent neighbor of ours put in a recommendation for a young job-seeker that led to his getting a great new job.

Recently I received a letter from a lady who recalled how her sister used to take walks in the country. As she strolled, she tossed sweet pea seeds along the road. Now countless people enjoy the lovely flowers that decorate the roadside.

Maybe you can mentor a young person, be a loyal friend, or volunteer for a worthy cause. Perhaps it's offering an inspiring word or letting someone know you believe in him or her. Give a genuine compliment, a smile, and a word of praise to those you meet along the way. Focus on the positive. Say something especially nice to the checkout person at the grocery store. Offer to carry a senior's groceries to his or her car.

Every day, let us show sincere love and appreciation to those around us, for that is what God wants us to do. God uses us to carry out His will, and one of the closest things to God's own heart is our acts of helping one another, for we are all His children.

Ever since my two older daughters began to talk, they have told me that when they get older they want to start an orphanage. With real feeling in their voices, they tell me, "We want to take care of the children who have no one to love and care for them."

Our girls have even picked out the location of the orphanage. There are three wooded acres about a mile from our home, and every time we drive past the land I say, "Girls, this is where the orphanage will be one day." In my mind, I see it coming to pass.

Lauren Grace, our oldest daughter, often declares, "Remember, Mom, when my sister and I are at work, you and Dad will care for the children until we get back."

My daughters' compassionate hearts remind me of the proverb that says, "One who is gracious to a poor man lends to the LORD, and He will repay him for his good deed" (Proverbs 19:17 NASB).

A short time ago I received a wonderful letter from a man who had an acquaintance who had reached the end of his rope. The man saw potential in his friend and so invested some time, money, and encouragement in him. The friend earned a degree and found a hope and satisfaction he'd long before despaired of.

I know this thoughtful man will be forever blessed by helping this person in need. His story takes me back to the Scripture "I will bless you . . . and you will be a blessing" (Genesis 12:2 NIV).

We can never do wrong by being good to others. Therefore, let us choose to focus on the theme *Live to Give*. Each morning, ask God to direct you to someone who needs your encouragement or assistance. Declare today, "I will be a light for others, and when they come in contact with me, I will do whatever I can to brighten their way."

Soon after Lauren Grace was born, I was at the doctor's office for a checkup. When I was leaving, the receptionist commented on the black-and-silver earrings I was wearing. "Those earrings are beautiful," she remarked. "Oh, I just love them."

Immediately, I took them off, handed them to her, and said,

"Here, you can have them." I thought, *This is the perfect opportunity*, for I try to do at least one good deed a day for someone. And the results I have experienced, when even one person says, "You've made me so happy," bring me real joy.

Looking at the shining earrings in my hand, the stunned receptionist asked, "What? You want me to have them?"

"Yes," I said, nodding. "Please, enjoy them."

"Are you sure, Catherine?" she questioned again.

"Positive," I confirmed, smiling.

With that, she reached out her hand and gratefully accepted them, still disbelieving what had just happened.

I will never forget the look of delight on the woman's face, or the joy I felt as I left the doctor's office that day. The path of a meaningful life is one of service. Giving can bring more happiness and fulfillment than anything else I know. Small, daily acts of kindness can invigorate our days and warm our hearts.

My friend told me a wonderful story about her kindhearted son. "We were in Boston visiting him when he was attending medical school, and we all went out for dinner. We had gone to his favorite restaurant in the Italian north end of Boston. Walking back from dinner, my son was holding two containers of food we hadn't been able to finish. His father and I had given them to him, knowing he often worked late at the hospital and missed dinner.

"We were passing through the walkway back from the North End, which leads to the market area. There were some homeless people sitting in the walk-thru. I assumed they would sit there and attempt to solicit people for money/donations or just for protection from the elements.

"As we were passing them, I saw my son look over at them,

but we kept walking. When I turned around to catch my son's eye, I saw that he was no longer with us. I asked myself, 'Where did he go?'" But I knew he had gone back to give the homeless people his food."

My friend told me that since then, whenever she goes out to eat with her son in Boston, they always get extra for him to give to any homeless people he might see.

Give anything and everything, whether it is time, money, a prayer, a hug, or a considerate word. It doesn't matter what the gift is; what matters is how much of ourselves goes into what we give.

A few years ago, after I had Sophia, I received a lovely note and a beautiful homemade multicolored blanket from Monica, a reader of my newspaper column who lives in Connecticut. Her mom had been skillful knitter of baby afghans, she said, and this was the very last one her mother made. I treasure this unconditional gift of love and will always remember Monica's kindness upon the birth of my daughter.

Look around you, and you'll find that there's a wonderful source of goodness in the universe, for we have been chosen to speak the reassuring word, to solve the problem, and to soothe the soul. True caring, kindheartedness, and love never fail. We may not see it outwardly or instantaneously, but a tiny seed of the love of God within us has been sown, and it will reap a great transformation, turning our lives and the lives of others into a beautiful, blessed experience.

NOTHING BREEDS OPTIMISM MORE THAN LOVE

In the seventeenth century, poet Thomas Stanley wrote his definition of success: "To leave the world a bit better, whether by a healthy child, a garden patch, or a redeemed social condition; to know that even one life has breathed easier because you have lived; this is to have succeeded."

What a wonderful philosophy of life! Isn't this really the essence of loving one another?

We strive for success because we seek material security and big bank accounts. But optimism is born when we receive a loving glance, hear the joyous laugh of a child, or receive a gesture of real caring.

We must comfort one another, strengthen and build one another up, and seize every opportunity to give hope to others. By sowing seeds of faith, hope, and love in others' hearts, we bring increase in abundance to our own.

I treasure the e-mail I received from an army private whose mother in the States sent him one of my columns. He said he appreciated the reminder of God's love and presence even in rough circumstances.

Have you ever noticed that God repeats the word *love* hundreds of times in His Scripture? For example:

- Love one another as I have loved you. (John 15:12 NKJV)
- Love your neighbor as yourself. (James 2:8 NIV)
- Be likeminded, having the same love, being of one accord, of one mind. (Philippians 2:2 KJV)
- If you love Me, keep My commandments. (John 14:15 NKJV)

I love the parable Jesus told about the good Samaritan. Recently I read this story to my young daughters. There was a man lying hurt and wounded on the roadside. A passerby walking on the opposite side of the road looked across toward the helpless man, but he did not cross over to the other side to assist him.

Another person came hurrying along, anxious to get out of the desolate area before nightfall. When he reached the wounded man, he turned away without offering any aid.

Then, along that lonely road came a man riding on his donkey, a Samaritan. He stopped immediately and ran to the man's side. *This man needs my help*, the Samaritan thought as he bound up the stranger's wounds and lifted him onto the back of his donkey.

The good Samaritan walked beside the poor man, holding him on his donkey until they reached the inn, and he cared for him all night. In the morning, when the Samaritan had to leave, he gave the landlord money and asked him to take care of the injured man. "And whatever more you spend," he said, " when I come again, I will repay you" (Luke 10:35 NKJV).

To support, comfort, and show kindness is like becoming a sheltering tree that enfolds all in its sweet shade. When we walk the road of life together, know that there will be burdens all along the way. But if we pray together, we will stay together beneath God's sheltering arms.

A week or so ago, with their fingers pointing to the sky, my daughters exclaimed, "Look, Mommy, look at all the geese!" Then they asked, "Why are they flying in a V shape?"

I replied, "They fly in a V formation to help one another. As each bird flaps its wings, it creates strength for the bird closely following. The flock of birds gains greater flying strength by flying together, because each goose gets help from the previous one. And they do not get as tired flying in a group."

What an awesome lesson God has given us by showing us the flight pattern of the geese. We, too, can support and uphold one another by sharing our prayers, nourish one another with encouragement, clothe ourselves in kindness, and by so doing, we will be brought together in a powerful new way.

HUMOR AND HEALTH ARE A PERFECT MATCH

There is a long-standing joke at our house and among my close friends. I tell them, "If things don't work out with my career, I am going to stay home, raise chickens, and sell the eggs in the street in front of my house."

Now, I'm only half kidding, because I love animals and nature. But you can banish tension, worry, and concern with laughter. If you smile, your burdens will be lightened. You probably don't think of laughter as medicine, but some believe it helps people live longer.

There is a direct correlation between humor and good health. Individuals who use laughter as a coping device in everyday life can have higher levels of infection-fighting antibodies. Like a bulletproof vest, laughter may help protect you against negative emotions by defusing anger. More and more evidence indicates that our thoughts, feelings, and attitudes not only play an obvious role in our mental health but are contributors to our physical well-being.

Gabriella is always twirling through the house. Every time you see her, she is giggling and twirling. I asked her, "Honey, why are you always spinning around?"

She replied, "I am so happy, I twirl!"

Well, maybe you won't be spinning through the house, but I heard that laughter has been called "inner jogging" because when we are engaged in a hearty laugh, the movement can help ease the stress in our organs. Laughing does not require any special equipment, clothing, or costs. It's readily accessible and free of charge, just waiting to burst out and brighten our day.

You might say, "I have too many problems to have a sense of humor." But did you know that humor is an incredible tool to use when you feel like crying? You can summon your sense of humor and gain strength when you feel powerless against the events in your life. It's at these times that humor can help smooth the rough edges and minimize things that you may find upsetting.

Humor helps keep things in perspective. I once overheard a person comment, "I am upset most of the time." Well, much of the anguish we experience is a result of how we view our problems. If we can laugh at an occasional stumbling block or use humor to help ease disappointments, we will no longer feel sorry for ourselves.

Instead, we will begin to feel uplifted and encouraged once again. Humor also draws our attention away from our difficulties. Rather than becoming glum, let's laugh at ourselves and at life. I take comfort in biblical wisdom: "Weeping may endure for a night, but joy cometh in the morning" (Psalm 30:5 KJV).

We can maintain a healthy balance by creating a "humor first-aid kit" to view whenever we need a good laugh. Fill your kit with humorous books, tapes, comics, and cartoons. Help bring laughter and smiles into others' lives by donating comic books or funny videos to your local hospital or library.

In our town, there is a restaurant my family likes to frequent on Thursday evenings. Why? Because on that night there is a magician who goes from table to table making funny-shaped balloons for the children and doing amusing magic tricks. The whole restaurant is alive with infectious laughter, and no matter their ages, people love the entertainment.

Laughter can ignite creativity, so make humor a habit. Set a time each day to focus on fun. Invite others to join in. One afternoon I was leaving the grocery store and an elderly man was walking behind me carrying a large pink bouquet. I turned around and said to him, "Oh, you shouldn't have. Thank you for these flowers. I love pink!" We both laughed, and his step had more of a spring to it as he walked on.

It's great to be around someone who laughs, announcing pleasure to others. Encourage a child's laughter, summon wit from your spouse, and ask older people to reminisce about happy memories.

I recall a conversation with Mary, who told me, "Catherine, I am having issues with a very opinionated coworker."

I said, "Remember, Mary, no person or circumstance can cause you to be unhappy unless you allow it."

Is somebody being critical or negative toward you? Don't buy into it; be too busy to be sad. Delight yourself in God and the talent He has given you.

I spoke to a gentleman who told me, "I am a kindergarten Sunday school teacher at the age of seventy-five. It keeps me young and full of glee." He realized that those sweet little ones still wear the shining robes of heaven's innocence and radiate God's pure countenance.

Whatever makes you laugh, put more of it into your life. Laughter is the music of the soul. Utilize this priceless gift of laughter and make the moments of your life even more precious.

NEVER UNDERESTIMATE THE
POWER OF ENTHUSIASM

As a unique individual, you must always express your enthusiasm to others. Scripture says, "Stir up the gift of God, which is in thee" (2 Timothy 1:6 KJV).

Real enthusiasm is an outward expression of inner joy. And often it distinguishes between the good and the great, the mediocre and the excellent.

I remember a movie classic that I watched years ago called *Pollyanna*. It is the touching story of a little girl whose parents were killed as missionaries, and she was sent to live with her aunt. But Pollyanna's optimistic attitude was contagious, and she helped change the lives of the people in the entire village.

In the movie, Pollyanna wore a locket around her neck—a locket that her father had given to her. Inside the locket was a quote from Abraham Lincoln. It read, "When you look for the bad in mankind expecting to find it, you surely will." Pollyanna went on to say, "After my father heard that quote he looked only for the good in people and made up the 'glad game.'" This was a game her father created to cover up the disappointments of his own life, trying to combat the negativity that can bombard one's mind.

Pollyanna also remembered her father saying, "If God took the trouble to tell us in the Bible eight hundred times to be 'glad' and happy, He must have wanted us to do it."

One secret of lasting enthusiasm, I believe, is to saturate our whole beings with, as Pollyanna said, the "glad" verses in the Bible. Put to memory sayings such as:

- ❧ The LORD is the strength of my life . . . in this I will be confident. (Psalm 27:1, 3 NKJV)
- ❧ Thou hast put gladness in my heart. (Psalm 4:7 KJV)
- ❧ Whatever things you ask in prayer, believing, you will receive. (Matthew 21:22 NKJV)
- ❧ Let us come before his presence with thanksgiving, and make a joyful noise unto him with psalms. (Psalm 95:2 KJV)
- ❧ He who is of a merry heart has a continual feast. (Proverbs 15:15 NKJV)
- ❧ As he thinketh in his heart, so is he. (Proverbs 23:7 KJV)

These phrases are like windows that open to a sun-filled dimension, showing us there is life beyond the momentary problems. Words from the Bible will help you keep your head up, your attitude positive, and your faith strong. Watch how your world changes as you add a "glad" verse to your memory.

Surround yourself with people who are glad. Encircle yourself with people who inspire you. I love to be around invigorating, encouraging, faith-filled people. Just being near them makes me more joyful.

A while back I met a business colleague who exemplified this philosophy. Leslie was warm, self-assured, and bursting with enthusiasm. When she walked up the driveway to our home, I heard her humming a tune, and when she looked at me the light in her eyes radiated happiness. Sitting at our kitchen table, sipping tea, I felt secure in her presence, and her energy and excitement were contagious!

"It's not your circumstances, it's your outlook," she told me, and after talking to her for just forty-five minutes, I was supercharged for days thereafter. It has now been months since I met her, and her passion, cheerfulness, and imagination still resonate within me.

A powerful transformation takes place when you are around enthusiastic people. They can help you attain your goals, motivate you into action, and inspire you to go higher. Encouraging, enthusiastic people are like flowers in the garden of life: they lend enchantment to everything ordinary.

Enthusiastic individuals are triumphant, victorious, and they regard nothing as impossible. And in spite of setbacks, they persist in their ambitions and visions with the fervent belief that they will come to pass.

I was impressed with a story I read about wildlife artist John James Audubon (1785–1851). One of the greatest naturalists America has ever produced, Audubon has a life story of triumph over adversity. A lover and observer of birds and nature, he was a man of legendary strength and endurance, driven by a deep appreciation for conservation.

Audubon would vanish into the wilderness for months, and when he returned he would have numerous precious drawings of birds. Once, after months of being away, he opened his truck where he had stored his cherished drawings and found that rats had gnawed at them, destroying his works of art.

Undaunted, Audubon professed to a friend, "They have destroyed my drawings, but not my enthusiasm." Thereafter, Audubon produced some of his greatest watercolors.

As the sun makes all of nature brighter, so do our lives become brighter with the inflowing of enthusiasm. For life's challenges cannot break one whose spirit is warmed by the dazzling rays of enthusiasm. They release the power to lift you above your obstacles and add power to all you do.

A lady friend once conducted an experiment. She was working as a cashier at a local department store. The long hours were tiring and she was drained, but her positive attitude and enthusiasm prevailed. Each person who came through her line received a warm smile and a genuine compliment or a kind word.

"Isn't this a great day?" she exclaimed to a weary senior, brightening her day.

"Your baby is precious. God bless him," she said to a new mother.

"What a beautiful dress you are wearing. You look lovely," she declared to another customer.

Soon, she said, she no longer felt listless; she was full of vitality and enthusiasm. Her customers left her line feeling happier, too.

Going through the motions can trigger feelings of happiness, and you can actually "act" yourself into a better frame of mind. When you apply love, you produce love! When you extend optimism, you produce positive outcomes every single time.

The world we live in is first shaped by the thoughts and attitudes we embrace. I believe our thought processes are creative, shaping us into who we will be for the rest of our lives. Those who are filled with enthusiasm and allow it to take hold will find new worlds open to them. Be inspired with a great purpose, come alive with enthusiasm, and put those great ideas into motion. Have confidence in the extraordinary individual you are and the positive influence you can be to others.

You can light your way to true peace, satisfaction, and success by turning to God and asking Him to open the doors He wants you to walk through with laughter, joy, love, and a great big smile, He will, you know. . . . He will.

LOOK FOR THE SILVER LINING

Todd and I were driving in the country one rainy Saturday afternoon when he suddenly pulled the car over to the side of the road. The rain was coming down so hard that visibility was poor. Thunder roared and lightning lit up the sky as the rain poured down in buckets.

"Look . . . isn't it beautiful?" Todd said enthusiastically as he pointed to the sky.

"What is?" I asked. "I don't see anything." I craned my neck to see out the window.

"It's over there," he said, reaching for an umbrella in the backseat and getting out of the car.

I stepped out, too, and went around to his side. In the distance, we saw it in all its glory: a magnificent rainbow, so big, so wide, so beautiful.

This experience made me think, *If I hadn't cared enough to get out of the car, even in the pouring, heavy rain, and take notice, I wouldn't have seen this spectacular vision.*

We have to care enough to look for the beauty in each day, search for the good, and rejoice in the best. If we don't, we'll miss it, as I might have missed the rainbow that day. It will pass us by and may be lost to us forever.

Though the sky may be rainy and the sun hidden from view by dark clouds, there are still treasures to be discovered. Do not give in to weakness and weariness—rise in your strength. Remember, the rainbow is a symbol of the promise of God. He gave it to Noah as a promise never to destroy the earth by flood again, as we read in Genesis 9:13–17.

God's Word is full of promises, so lift your eyes and look

for the rainbow. It will brighten your heart, dry your tears, and restore your faith.

Here is the key. Get into the habit of looking for the silver lining of the storm clouds and focus on the beauty of life—and you will surely find it. Don't let anyone else put blinders on your soul. Do not be discouraged, no matter how distressed you are or how confusing things appear to be. Look for the rainbow. Your sorrow will vanish deep in the center of each gorgeous hue.

I once wrote a column that included these words: "Stop telling God how big your storm is; instead, tell your storm how big God is!" One woman read those words just prior to undergoing a double mastectomy. Now celebrating five years of health, she shares that same attitude with friends who need strength.

Say aloud the following Scripture verses: "My God shall supply all [my] need according to His riches in glory by Christ Jesus" (Philippians 4:19 NKJV); or "Come to Me, all you who labor and are heavy laden, and I will give you rest" (Matthew 11:28 NKJV); or "Be strong and of good courage, do not fear nor be afraid . . . for the LORD your God, He is the One who goes with you" (Deuteronomy 31:6 NKJV).

The bigger you make God, the smaller your problems become. Each promise is a rainbow designed from the heart of the Father's love, and that love is always with you, whatever the circumstances may be.

He will take you by the hand, stand by your side, and see you through difficult times. How wonderful it is that we can look to a loving Father who will take care of us.

Trust Him, enjoying each day; and look ahead, expecting wonderful things to materialize. God has an assignment for you to accomplish. He is a miracle worker, and He knows what He is doing. Psalm 16:8 says, "I know the LORD is always with me. I will not be shaken, for he is right beside me" (Psalm 16:8 NLT).

A happy person is not a person in a certain set of circumstances, but rather someone with a certain set of attitudes. Continually look up to God. Happiness is being aware of His great love for you. Cheerfulness is a natural attribute of that awareness.

You have the ability to choose your responses in any given situation. Nothing of value in life ever comes easily. Life is a testing time. You can never pass the test without studying the Book and knowing the promises. Believing in them will get you an A+.

I saw this firsthand when my friend was diagnosed with a tumor in her inner ear. Week after week, she had to undergo numerous tests. Then came the chemotherapy and radiation. Through the entire ordeal, she was continually faithful, upbeat, and optimistic about the outcome.

She prayed and believed without a doubt that God was with her and would see her through. And she kept her mind focused positively on her job, family, and helping others, never dwelling on her sickness. Months later, when my friend went for her follow-up doctor visit, she was declared well. It has been five years now, and she is completely healthy and strong.

God has given you the extraordinary power to choose the way you think, act, and achieve. Trust in the goodness of God. A strong, faith-filled, optimistic outlook will help you feel better through a medical crisis, whatever the physical outcome.

This evening I was sitting on my bed reading. Next to me was Gabriella. Out of the blue, my daughter said, "Mom, there are ten words I always keep in my mind."

Curious, I asked, "Honey, what are the ten words?"

She replied, "Whatever we do . . . everything is going to turn out great."

Now that is true optimism!

OPTIMISM:
Key to Your Heart's Desire

○—⚷ We all want to know the secret to happiness. But the secret to truly enjoying life lies in having the right attitude in our hearts. It is all about *how we choose to see life.* So joyfully expect the best. Speak positive words, think positive thoughts, and take positive action.

○—⚷ Time is one of our most important possessions. And today offers at least sixteen waking hours that can be utilized to the fullest, packed full of enthusiasm, possibilities, and the opportunity to positively influence others. Make the most of this time.

○—⚷ Like the wheels on a car, adversities have their part and purpose. They carry us forward to achieving new wisdom.

○—⚷ Keeping a vibrantly optimistic attitude means being constantly on guard against negativity. Success and creativity grow and flow only in a positive, upbeat atmosphere. Only we can create this atmosphere and must build a strong defense around it.

⚬—⚔ Be happy with who God created you to be. You are a valuable, significant, and exceptional human being. Practice the happiness habit. Decide at this moment you will be optimistic regardless of circumstances.

⚬—⚔ Just because your heart's desires have not happened yet doesn't mean they won't. The seasons do not hurry themselves; nor do the trees, which grow so high and tall. To everything there is a season, and all things transpire at their own paces. Keep expecting the best. Who can tell what fantastic opportunities lie ahead?

⚬—⚔ We must keep in continual contact with God, our great positive force. To truly be creative, we must always place our eyes upon His loving-kindness. We must continue to invigorate our spirits by speaking only words that are pure, pleasant, constructive, and affirmative.

Key #4:
HOPE

"I know the plans I have for you," declares the
Lord, "plans to prosper you and not to harm you,
plans to give you hope and a future."

(Jeremiah 29:11 NIV)

Suppose a wise mentor said to you, "I have uncovered one of life's most powerful secrets. It is a tool that will help you throughout your life."

What would you say? Immediately you'd probably ask, "What is it? I'd love to know how I can get it!"

In this chapter, you will discover this secret, for I believe there is no power greater than hope, no incentive as great, and no tonic as strong as the joyful expectation of a better tomorrow. Hope is *absolute joyful expectation* created by our faith in God, for God is hope.

What can you do to embark upon this new way of living? The key is to start by thinking hopeful thoughts, expressing hopeful words, and initiating hope-filled actions.

Adopt an attitude that radiates a belief in the power of hope. Be joyful and confident. You will find that with hope in your heart you can overcome any obstacle, conquer any problem, and accomplish every dream.

One of my favorite Scriptures is this: "The steadfast love of the LORD never ceases, his mercies never come to an end; they are new every morning" (Lamentations 3:22–23 RSV).

In view of that beautiful promise, behold the bright dawn of a new day and move on to a triumphant future. There are innumerable blessings and wonderful possibilities for you just ahead. . . . New every morning, the sun shines brightly on a clean page in the book of your life.

Join with me, and atop each page of your book of life, write the word *hope*.

LEARN TO OVERCOME WITH GOD'S STRENGTH, NOT JUST YOUR OWN

With hope in your heart, you can triumph over any obstacle in life. The key is to rely on God's strength rather than your own. A dear friend says, "When I don't know what to do, I pray, 'God, take care of this for me,' and He always does."

Today, put down the burdens you are holding. Break away from the hurt, let go of the pain, and release the mistakes of long ago. Take the wisdom learned from past experiences and spring forward with rekindled hope. Put all the happiness and enjoyment you can into each moment, and look forward to the blessings yet to be.

Try a viewpoint like this: *I will look out on this day and every day with the enthusiasm of a child, with the strength of a youth, and with the wisdom of a grandparent.* Each day is a new beginning.

Think about the immensity of the desert as it stretches out with red rock canyons, sand, and sage. Each year, suddenly and briefly, flowers actually bloom in the desert. With little warning, it is transformed into a cascade of golds, reds, and greens.

Would you like the desert of your life to undergo a similar transformation? All you need to do is, with renewed hopefulness, start this day with joyful expectation. Remember, no matter what has happened in your life, God wants to give you a fresh start, a new hope, and a brighter future.

After my mother died, I found myself living alone, destitute, in a tiny two-room apartment in one of the worst sections of the city. Often I drove about forty minutes to the shoreline, walked along the beach, and dreamed about one day being happy.

I loved the beach, and I would gaze out at the vast blue ocean and listen to the cry of the seagulls as they soared overhead. As I walked on the sand, along the ocean's edge, I would affirm to myself: *I know God has a plan for me. There must be a purpose for all this. This, too, shall pass.*

With each step, I'd quietly affirm, *I'll ignore the obstacles in front of me and keep my eyes on my goals ahead. I have what I need to succeed. Follow your heart, Catherine. Today, I will lift up someone in need.*

On and on I went. "Thank You, God for my life," I prayed. "With Your help, Lord, I will turn my dreams into reality." And then to myself: *I will be happy. I'll keep trying.*

What was I doing? I was getting my hopes up again by bringing myself to a place where I could dream—the ocean. And it was those God-given dreams and sincere hopes for a better future that gave me the strength to carry on. When it was time to leave the beach, I always felt more energized, focused, and hopeful.

You, too, must fill your soul with encouraging affirmations, positive thoughts of hope, and joyful expectations, so that they outweigh and outrun the negative.

Please don't ever let another person spoil your bright plans or aspirations. Forget the negativity of others. It does not matter what people try to do to hinder us, hurt us, or mistreat us. Our destinies are ordered by an all-powerful God, and He has plans for us to triumph. Take it from me: the underdog can win!

So don't hide from your problems. Instead, push on to a higher cause, because with God on your side, you will succeed. I like to recall what David said in Psalm 23: "I will fear no evil: for thou art with me; thy rod and thy staff they comfort me" (Psalm 23:4 KJV).

Sometimes we think about what we don't have. You may say, "I don't have the connections or the resources I need to do well." But here is the key: do you know that hidden within you is the person God planned for you to be when you were born? What an incredible fact! Do not underestimate your strength, your worth, or your potential!

I once read that Dr. Martin Luther King Jr. considered Dr. Benjamin Mays his spiritual leader. This clergyman was a wonderful source of inspiration. He once said, "Whatever you do, do it so well that people looking on will feel that the task was reserved especially for you by God Himself."

Lift up your eyes from where you are, take a deep breath, and pour out to God your desires. He is a Creator, and He is always creating something wonderful. Get His nod of approval in your heart and open your arms to receive the Lord's joy. This will be your strength.

I was so inspired by a letter from one of my readers—a truly remarkable woman! She wrote that at the age of fifty-four she transitioned from a law career to a new one in health care. She admitted that listening to God's guidance and acting on His direction required an enormous leap of faith. Yet the rewards were so satisfying! With God in your corner, you can do anything!

Like this amazing woman, we, too, must remember that we are the Lord's precious children, and He loves us unconditionally. As we choose to remain hopeful and serve God, no matter what challenges arise, God will honor us, and in due season He will reward our faithfulness.

When situations appear unfair or uncertain, I take the position of hopefulness because I believe that who I am and who I become are not determined by my circumstances. The outcome of my life will be determined by how I think. I have found that when I hold on to hope, God may use a difficult situation to bring me to a new place of victory.

One evening recently, we lost power in our house. Our entire neighborhood lay in darkness after a raging windstorm. Taken by surprise, Todd hurried downstairs to find a flashlight while I searched the cabinets for a candle. The girls ran to the window to look outside at the night sky. Then Gabriella, wide-eyed with awe, said, "Mommy, we never saw the stars shine so big and bright until the lights went out, did we?"

How true! I thought. Sometimes darkness offers us the perfect opportunity to discover the radiance of the stars and allows us to understand things we might not otherwise experience. Problems can actually open the door to new opportunities for us, so it's more important than ever to look for the light when darkness seems to be all around us.

Did you know the Bible reveals that our faith is "much more precious than gold" (1 Peter 1:7 NKJV)? It is in difficult situations that our faith is strengthened, lessons are learned, and character traits are developed. Think about how sparkling diamonds are produced. First they are formed under great pressure. Then their beauty is created by cuts and blows to the stone. Isn't it interesting that often great men and women are also formed this way?

I once heard it said, "The person who can smile when everything seems to go against him shows that he or she is made of winning material."

A gentleman told me a short time ago that his company had a financial crisis and laid him off. But he remained hopeful and prayerful and said he expected a new job to appear soon. He praised God for His faithfulness despite the difficulties of unemployment.

Throughout life, we may not understand why some things happen, so we have to trust God and pray for His will to be done. Sometimes our prayers are not answered right away and the world seems filled with silence. Then God's voice within us can once again be heard, and we are reminded once more that He is always working His grand design in our lives. Scripture says, "Be of good courage, and he shall strengthen your heart, all ye that hope in the LORD" (Psalm 31:24 KJV).

Are you facing a challenging situation today? If so, let me ask you this: What if you knew that you would be brought out of it successfully within a short period of time? Would you continue to be worried or upset? Of course not—you would rest easy.

Please, do that now and turn your unsolved problems, your dreams, and your aspirations completely over to God. There is no need to fear when we put our hope and faith in Him, for He will raise us up and bring peace to our hearts.

WITH HOPE, ANYTHING IS POSSIBLE

As long as we have hope in our hearts, we cannot be defeated. Isn't that the truth?

Hope is like the sun: as we journey toward it, the shadows of our burdens are cast behind us. We may be hurt, but with hope, we will not be beaten. We may experience times of despair, but with hope, we will not give in to discouragement. When circumstances look futile, with hope, we will not concede. With hope, we will weather the roughest storms.

Long ago I read the story of a soldier who was severely wounded on the battlefield. A medical doctor said, "If this man can live until tomorrow's sun goes down, he will get well."

The soldier heard what the doctor uttered, and his words of hope lingered in his mind. As he clung tenaciously to life, the soldier repeated those words to himself: *If I can live until tomorrow's sun goes down, I will get well.*

Believing this to be so, he watched the sun rise and again set. And the soldier miraculously did survive.

Every one of us has the ability to make another person stronger and responsive to our words. If we choose to speak with hope and optimism, we can positively affect those around us. In fact, we can even change another person's life.

Some time ago, a reader wrote telling me about her dear sister, a third-grade teacher who noticed one of her students was struggling academically. She saw his clear intelligence and a potentially bright future, so she pulled him aside one day and told him she knew he could be one of her best students. Stunned and inspired, the boy worked to improve in all the areas that challenged him and even took on extra assignments. He did indeed become her top student and eventually succeeded throughout his school years. Giving the boy words of support and encouragement transformed his life.

Everyone needs hope, and when someone has confidence in our abilities, we can sometimes achieve miraculous results. What is the key? We must look for ways each day to comfort, strengthen, and build one another up.

I know a woman who was just leaving the hospital after visiting her sick child. A parking garage guard saw that she had been crying and offered her these comforting words: "Have hope. Things will work out all right, you'll see." Those words helped her so much that the woman vowed that every day, she would say one kind word or do one good deed for someone else.

If we seize every opportunity to give hope and encouragement, we can make a difference in someone's life just as someone can make a difference in ours. I remember a day back in the early nineties when I walked into a photo shop one cold winter afternoon. I was picking up some pictures and feeling pretty glum. I felt as if I had the world on my shoulders as I struggled with mounting bills and a life filled with uncertainty.

While I was awaiting my turn, I noticed the man behind the counter write a few words on a pink sticky note, and then to my surprise, he handed it to me. The man's name was David, and I had seen him only a few times before. A bit startled, I took the sticky note from him and looked at the words on the small piece of paper. It read, "You are wonderful and deserve every good thing that happens good to you."

I can't begin to describe what those words meant to me . . . and still mean to me. Even now, as I am sharing this story with you, my eyes fill with tears. I clung to that note, reading it time and again, and allowing it to become a beacon of light in my then-dark world.

Today, I still carry that pale pink note with me in my day planner. And from time to time, I take it out and remember David, the man with the kind words I will never forget.

I sometimes wonder if we really understand how powerful our words can be. We can program our minds to focus on only the most nurturing, strengthening, and wholesome ideas.

"How?" you might ask. Let me answer with a question: how

often do you speak quickly, without giving thought to the force and impact of your words?

Do you want to try this test? For three days (seventy-two hours), say only positive things. Express only words of love, hope, good wishes, positive remarks, and genuine admiration. I know a woman named Maria who tried this and reported, "Catherine, by just changing my speech, I noticed a profound difference in the way I felt, how I behaved, and consequently what I accomplished."

Remember: speak only of good for three days straight. And then . . . see what happens. Are you all set to begin?

When I pass on compliments to my sweet daughters, their faces glow. As I praise my husband for being such a great husband and father to our children, my reward is seeing his eyes light up. While I console a dear friend and express compassion for her problems, her tears are replaced with a grateful smile.

We all are creators, in a fashion, just like our Father. We create by the words that come out of our mouths. Our voices' potential for good is boundless.

At work, create a warm family atmosphere and let a spirit of good fellowship flow toward everyone who works with you. A friendly "Good morning" or "You've done a great job" can do wonders.

My daughter Lauren informed me that in her fourth-grade class they have a morning "compliment greeting." When I asked her what that meant, she explained that each child says something complimentary to his or her fellow classmate, such as: "Good morning, Amanda, I like your dress," or "Happy Monday, Sam, I think you have a good sense of humor," or "Hi, Julia, you are a great softball player." The children love this, and it teaches them to pass on kindnesses and compliments.

If it works for our children, it can work for us, too. Every day, resolve to use expressions of hope, appreciation, reassurance, and genuine affection. Let people know that you care about them. A friend of mine said with a chuckle that she always wanted to wear a button that reads "Smile when you talk to me—I'm paranoid." None of us are mind readers, and when we see someone smile at us, we know we are special.

I like to write thank-you notes to people who have touched my life with kindness. Sometimes I bring them a small gift. If someone is going through a difficult time or if I want someone to know I appreciate him or her, I'm partial to sending what I call "A Book of Love." These are actual books that you can purchase and display in your home, as they are made to stay open, and written in them is warm, loving sentiment.

Do you feel good when you put your house in order and when the rooms are neat and clean? I am a very organized, structured person, and I must organize my notes and arrange my office and desk perfectly before I start writing or designing. Otherwise I cannot create.

There is another kind of clutter, and that comes from negative thoughts and words. I know it is our nature to want to tell others our problems. I like to talk to my wise friend as well, to get her sensible opinion about certain situations. However, once we share our concern with that one special friend and come to a conclusion about it, we must leave it alone and not speak of the issue again. By rehashing our dilemmas repeatedly, we exaggerate them, and this serves only to accentuate our unhappiness.

Instead, let's cite life-affirming, hopeful phrases such as:

- I am just being challenged.
- Life is full of adventures.

- ❧ I will get better.
- ❧ I can do that!
- ❧ I'll keep hoping.
- ❧ I am thankful for all my blessings.
- ❧ God loves me.

Write these phrases down and post them where you can see them every day.

Hope and perseverance triumph and open the door to success. Hope pushes ahead when it would be easy to quit. Perseverance together with hope can bring new achievement!

As we travel through life, let us create hope for both ourselves and others. The possession of hope is, in itself, happiness. That arching rainbow of pure hope can lift us higher than we could imagine and help us press on to greater heights and achievements.

RISE ABOVE INJUSTICE WITH HOPE AND FAITH

What we achieve does not matter as much as how we achieve it.

"In life, you are given three names," wrote Abraham Lincoln. "One you inherit, one you are given by your parents, and one you make for yourself."

I believe who we become in the process of living is key to what we achieve while we're still here on this beautiful earth. The character we acquire, the lessons we learn, the people we influence, and the heart of hope and compassion we possess are legacies we carry with us and then pass on to our loved ones.

What we set our sights on determines who and what we will become. So let us set our sights on excellence, allowing it to encompass all areas of our lives. When we do the right thing and try our best, even when situations are difficult or unfair, God will honor our intentions and our efforts.

For many months, a childhood friend of mine was suffering from tremendous stress and strain. Through no fault of her own, she had become involved in a venture with someone who was abusive, degrading, and trying to sabotage her thriving career. It was heartbreaking and maddening for me to watch this, as my friend is a giving, honest person. She worked tirelessly, spending many years on this endeavor. But as time went on, the situation was not improving, and the negativity that surrounded it was beginning to affect her health and home life.

She called me one afternoon and tearfully explained her dilemma.

"Pray, for the Lord is with you," I encouraged. "You must do a lot of soul-searching and think about what you really want. Concentrate on your needs and your family's needs. That is what really counts."

I also told her that God had not brought her this far to give up on her now. "The Lord sees how hard you work, your dedication and pure motives, and how unfairly you have been treated. He has a plan. Trust Him to work this out for you."

Merciful and just, God will vindicate us. When He sees the wrongs, the hurts, and unjust circumstances that have victimized us, He will come forward in His time and repay every injustice we have borne.

In addition, I told my friend, "Persist in creating new plans. Dream some new dreams, think bigger, and write down on a sheet of paper a revised goal list. Focus on that instead of on the dilemma about which you can do nothing right now."

So that is what she did. She expanded her thoughts, refocused her goals, and made a list of dreams that would allow her to spend more time with her family and, in the process, help others. Then she visualized exciting new plans coming to pass and began to expect positive results. She forced all thoughts of failure out of her mind and refused to be pulled down by adverse conditions.

A few weeks later, my friend called me, overjoyed.

"What happened?" I asked.

"Today I was offered a major contract with an international company. And this very same day, out of the blue, a former business associate telephoned me and invited me to New York City to meet a colleague of hers who's interested in my work."

When my friend explained to me the turnaround of events in her life, I was reminded of the Scriptures:

> Instead of your shame
> you shall have double honor,
> And instead of confusion
> they shall rejoice in their portion.
> Therefore in their land they shall possess double;
> Everlasting joy shall be theirs. (Isaiah 61:7 NKJV)

> You prisoners of hope . . . even today I declare that I will
> restore double to you. (Zechariah 9:12 NKJV)

This weekend is my daughters' dance recital. Lauren and Gabriella, under the direction of the dance teacher, have spent months practicing and preparing for their ballet and tap routines. Now, before the curtain opens for the Saturday performance, the set design is in place, the music is ready to be played, the lighting is perfected, and the dancers are in position to begin their opening number. It takes time to get everything in order. But when all is completely in place, the curtain will open to the sound of applause, and the marvelous show will begin.

In our lives, it takes time for God to arrange things in perfect sequence. I like to think of it this way: *hope sees the hidden design.*

My memories take me back to a nice couple we know, Kate and Mark. Mark had been out of work for three years. After twenty years of devoted service in the food industry, his job had been eliminated. Dejected, he felt he would never find another career as lasting and satisfying as his last one had been.

To assist with the mounting expenses, Kate took on extra hours at her job. She tried her best to comfort and console her husband. She urged him, "Things will be okay. Just keep your hope alive. And have faith, because God will take care of us."

She also prepared him for better times. "Soon, you will be ushered into a great new career," she would tell him.

However, month after month passed and nothing happened. Mark searched the want ads daily, sent out résumés, went to interviews, and continued getting rejected.

Then something changed: Mark's attitude. The catalyst was deciding not to give up, closing the door on fear and worry, and opening the window to faith and hope. Instead, he began speaking about what God could and would do, sensing for the first time that God was right by his side.

While he continued his job search, he was drawn to start volunteering at his church. He enjoyed helping members in need and also liked spending more time with his grown daughters and extended family. Mark said, "I believe if I keep doing good things, God's timing will send good back to me."

One day, Kate was at her exercise class. She had been going to this class a few times a week for years. On this particular day, a woman she barely knew walked up to her before the class began.

The two women started talking. "My husband, Mark, is doing well," confided Kate, "even though he's been out of work for some time." Then she told her new friend a little about their present situation.

Suddenly, the woman, a virtual stranger, said, "Kate, maybe I can help him. Ask your husband to e-mail me his résumé."

After the exercise class, the woman wrote down her e-mail address on a tiny slip of paper and handed it to Kate. Kate was a bit startled. "Well, thank you," she said. "I really appreciate any help you can give us."

That evening, when Kate got home, she passed the woman's message on to her husband. "Honey," she said, "I don't even know why I confided in this woman about your career situation, because I don't know her that well, but it seemed natural for me to tell her a little about what we've been going through."

"That's fine," Mark said, looking at the sheet of paper with the woman's e-mail address on it. "I'll send her my résumé tomorrow. You just never know. . . ."

Within a week, Mark had an interview with a large newspaper group. Three weeks later, he was hired as part of their sales department, starting a great new career. Now, two years later, Mark is one of the top sales executives in the organization.

Maybe, as Kate's husband felt at one time, you are about to give up hope. But stand strong, continue trying, be patient, and keep your sights high! Someone out there may well be on his or her way to help you, too.

It's been said that we are each writing a gospel, a page a day, with the words we speak, the deeds we perform, and the actions we choose. God has a special phrase for us: "My beloved child." As we move forward in hope and faith, He is waiting to bestow His blessings upon us.

WHERE THERE'S LIFE, THERE'S HOPE

Do you feel overwhelmed and defeated? Does everything appear to be at a standstill? Do you want to give up?

Before you do, take a deep breath and then declare, as my mother used to say, "Where there's life, there's hope."

We must never lose hope, our beacon through rough times. We never know when our circumstances will turn around and, in an instant, take us in a wonderful new direction.

It's easy to be hopeful when everything is going well. But what kind of outlook do we have when things don't go our way? Do we stay expectant? Will we keep pressing forward?

Actually, when we're hopeful, we see each stumbling block as a stepping-stone. We know we must continue on our quest, so we get back up, dust ourselves off, and keep trying. Hope pushes us forward when it would be very easy to say, "I've had enough."

One afternoon I was driving to a restaurant to meet a friend for lunch. She had been depressed and wanted to talk to me. She confided on the phone that recent situations had gone poorly for her, and she just didn't know what to do.

As I walked into the dining room of the restaurant, I saw my friend sitting at the table, looking distressed, her hand on her forehead.

I went over to the table, gave her a hug, and then sat across from her. "What's wrong?" I asked, concerned by her troubled appearance.

For the next thirty minutes, she described in full detail all the difficulties she had encountered in her relationship, including scores of regrets. She felt so weighed down by self-doubt; she felt she was losing faith in both God and herself.

When she finished, I thought about everything she'd shared with me and then said, "You know, even though certain plans didn't work out, this is not the end—it's actually the beginning of a new direction in your journey. Push aside those roadblocks of regret, apply what you've learned, and move forward by taking positive action."

My friend nodded. "Catherine, I know, but it is so difficult."

Leaning toward her, I whispered, "God loves you, and if you ask, He'll give you the strength to overcome this challenge. Don't lose hope or faith in Him." Then I had a thought. What would my mother advise? As if she were right there next to me I received her words, which I passed on to my friend: "Remember, wherever there is life, hope also dwells."

I saw a glimmer of hope in my friend's eyes, so I reached for her hand and began telling her a story I have always loved that has given me great comfort during difficult times.

The title of the story is "Footprints in the Sand," and it was written by Mary Stevenson. In the narrative, a man has a dream that he is walking with God along the beach and God shows him flashbacks of his life. During these flashbacks, the man sees that sometimes there were two sets of footprints in the sand, one set representing God and the other his own. However, at times there was only one set of footprints. These occurred during the most difficult and heartbreaking situations the man had endured.

The man asked God, "Why was there only one set of footprints at the most difficult times in my life?" God tenderly replied, "I love you and I would never leave you. When you see only one set of footprints, it was then that I carried you."

Moved by these words about God's love, my friend began to weep quietly. Deep within, she recognized the wisdom of this tale and knew she would never be alone.

Dear readers, there is always hope. Sometimes there seems to be no logical solution to your predicaments. You may be confronted with a dilemma that looks hopeless, and you might not be able to see an answer—today. But you can prevail over these times because with God and hope as your allies, there is nothing you cannot overcome, no hurt you cannot forgive, and no difficulty you cannot conquer.

If you are going through a trial, know that God is carrying you right now. At times you may not feel that you can take another step. Just know there is nothing in life that you and God cannot conquer together!

Many months have passed since that early afternoon luncheon, and I am happy to report that my friend's issues were all resolved. But to this day, she tells me that whenever she finds herself thinking of defeat, she immediately changes her thoughts to: *Wherever there is life, hope also dwells.*

When we are faced with a situation that seems overwhelming, we need to remember how small it is compared to the power of our magnificent God.

IT'S NEVER TOO LATE TO ACHIEVE
YOUR DREAMS

Are there aspirations in your heart that you have let go? Do you have an ambition that you are yearning to fulfill?

Young or old, rich or poor, up or down, if you have a dream, you can reach it.

What is it that you really want? You can have it. . . . It is never too late.

God made each one of us unique, with no two sets of fingerprints alike. He made each one of us for a divine and individual purpose.

At this very moment, imagine yourself alone with the Creator of the universe, who pulled from His Spirit an original work of art when He designed you. On His easel, He placed the canvas of your unique self. The paint used was the rainbow of His glorious character, and each bristle of the brush was alive with unconditional love. Using precise placement, expert skill, and great compassion, God made you to be a masterpiece.

Stop now, and take a few minutes to ponder this awesome fact: you are a masterpiece, a fabulous work of art. Consider paintings by Rembrandt, Monet, or Hofmann. They have great value because they were created by masters, and each is a priceless work of art. You were created by the greatest Master, God Himself, in His own image. What an awesome fact is this!

You are, to Him, the most valuable object on earth, and the longer you live, the greater your experience and wisdom.

No matter your age, social status, situation, or job, you can strive to be the best. There is a power within you can tap. If you think right, you can rise above any situation and be a success in life.

People have written to me, saying, "Catherine, I have made too many mistakes. I feel unworthy." Start by reprogramming your mind to forget disappointments and failures. A senior friend of mine says with a chuckle, "This should be easy because forgetting is natural as you get older." Start living for today only, embrace the hope God offers you, and see if you can't make this today a little better than yesterday.

"But Catherine," you might say, "where do I begin?"

Try starting a file and stuff it with pictures of dreams you may have discarded: a home filled with people to love, an exciting new business, an exhilarating hobby, a beloved pet, or a peaceful vacation. Tear pictures out of old magazines. Collect them to remind yourself that the future is filled with unlimited possibilities.

Imagine viewing your life when you're one hundred years old. What will you wish you had done differently? Organize your priorities with one-hundred-year-old hindsight. Everyone can start again and anew no matter what age. It is only a thought away.

After working in a dissatisfying job for forty-three years, a fifty-nine-year-old woman went back to school. Despite the rigorous academic demands, she and her prayer partners claimed victory. Though she continued to struggle with school, and her husband endured a battle with cancer and a period of unemployment, this woman praises God for His abundant answers to prayer. She feels strongly she's pursuing the career God designed for her and confident He will see her through all the obstacles.

I'm acquainted with a couple who have been married for fifty years. Instead of thinking about downsizing their home, they recently expanded, purchasing a two-acre estate!

An unforgettable gentleman I know is nearing ninety. He still works as an accountant, does all his own yard work and home repairs, and helps with the neighbor children.

A woman in town, at eighty-five, volunteers at the school, reading with students.

Your mind is a brilliant machine, and you can program it for success and happiness by cultivating a love and appreciation for people and life. You have something valuable to do, and so, in the words of Henry Wadsworth Longfellow, "Let us, then, be up and doing"!

An eighty-three-year-old songwriter wrote to tell me that one of his songs was being distributed in Nashville and that he had been hired to write more songs. He recommends that you keep asking, seeking, knocking. Eventually the right door will open!

History is filled with stories of older individuals who continued to be creative well into their senior years. Albert Schweitzer was still lovingly treating patients when he was ninety. Thomas Edison was still inventing when he was eighty. Picasso worked until he was ninety. And Michelangelo was painting Saint Peter's in Rome at age eighty-eight.

Each year is an added opportunity for adventure. Each year you have a choice: walk in hope, or walk in despair.

Not long ago a lady friend told me, "Through prayer and belief in God's plan for me, life has a quality of meaning I had never experienced during the first fifty years of my life." Sometimes we have to redirect our lives, for we are never too old to learn. Each moment should hold the bright window of learning, because God never stops teaching.

So come alive with creativity. Create joy for someone. Inspiration for creativity comes when you are full of desire to enrich someone else's life. You can get enthused about life again.

Your good deeds do not have to be elaborate. Run errands for a neighbor, let another driver merge in front of you, pass along a good book to a coworker, put a coin in an expired meter, say "Thank you," offer to help a busy mom, bring a batch of cookies to work, give out hugs and positive praise at home, and tell those special people in your life how much they mean to you.

How about this idea? Start a collection . . . of smiles! Begin a "cheer-up phone service." Call shut-ins or others who need a cheerful word. Gather their responses and write down the results daily. After a while, you may have a best seller in the making.

One of the books on a shelf in my office is titled *Streams in the Desert* by Mrs. Charles Cowman. First published in 1925, the idea of the book came from Mrs. Cowman's bedridden husband, a pastor. His desire to help others could not be quenched even during his years of inactivity. Since then, it has sold millions of copies and encouraged people from all walks of life with its depths of compassion and understanding. Even today, its message is surprisingly timely.

So give a gift to the world. Pick up your dream and start today with a hope-filled heart. Pray and begin. You will find it undeniably bears the stamp of the Supreme Creator's divine touch.

THE PATH MAY BE DARK, BUT WITH HOPE YOU CAN DRIVE OUT FEAR

One of the greatest achievements in life is to overcome, to triumph over obstacles, fears, resentments, and limitations. And how do we do this? I found the answer in the Bible, for it is the Word of God. In Psalms we read, "The LORD is my light and my salvation—whom shall I fear? The LORD is the stronghold of my life—of whom shall I be afraid?" (Psalm 27:1 NIV).

The presence of problems is a part of life. We must not be overwhelmed but instead handle them with courage and faith. During our most difficult moments, we all have the opportunity to have faith in God, keep our hearts filled with hope, and let go of our fears.

When Renee, a dear relative of ours, was battling the rare disease of scleroderma, which has no known cure, she expressed only hope each time we spoke. I would call her every day and she would always say, "Catherine, when I get well, I may get another cat." "Once I improve, I'll drive again." "When I'm up and around, I will plant those flowers." "As soon as I am feeling better, I will get my appetite back."

I never heard her complain even once. Her concern was always for others. Despite being very sick, Renee made plans and looked to the future with hope. Her days were filled with the knowledge that God was with her and would carry her through to a better tomorrow.

It's true what Carl Sandburg wrote in his book about Abraham Lincoln: "A tree is best measured when it is down." Our lives are measured not when all is going right, but when we are toppled by trials and difficulties. What kind of people are we then? Are we still kind and gentle with others? Do we hold on to hope?

In my search for the meaning of our existence, I found the answer by seeking a personal relationship with God. Through Him I have found the strength to persist, abiding faith to continue, and boundless hope during life's difficult times. With Him, there is abundant joy, deep peace, and true contentment.

When the sting of pain, hurt, and heartache overwhelms us, we must seek God and know that we are loved. As we cast our burdens upon Him, He will comfort us, grant us serenity, and uphold us.

Jesus told us, "My yoke is easy and My burden is light" (Matthew 11:30 NKJV). (In the time of Jesus, a yoke was a piece of wood placed across the back of two oxen to join them so they could work together.) In the same way, God's Word holds us in line so we can receive the blessings that obeying His Word brings. Obeying His Word may not be the easiest way, but it lifts our heaviest burdens and makes them light. By doing so, we can understand these words of Jesus: "Come, take up the cross, and follow Me" (Mark 10:21 NKJV).

Some time ago, I received a letter from a reader whose story so inspired me it brought me to tears. She had suffered unimaginable losses: her home had burned down, and she lost her son and everything she owned in the fire. Rather than letting loss steal her faith, though, she kept trusting God and now ministers to other bereaved parents. She shares the same life and hope she received with others who desperately need it.

Another reader was diagnosed with a serious degenerative disease. Though severely challenged, she holds on to hope and listens for God's guidance. A close and comforting relationship with Him is the result.

I look out my window and see a break in the clouds as sunshine spills onto the earth. Even so I wonder, *Why are trials allowed? For what purpose must we go through the things that we do?*

Then a deep sense of inner peace comes as the answer becomes astonishingly clear. Within my heart, I hear the Lord say, "The footsteps of the righteous are ordered by the Lord. I am here. I am with you. I am your Protector and your Provider. Those who believe and are in need, do not fear, do not worry . . . for your God is with you."

A few nights ago, I woke up at 2 a.m. A situation had been on my mind, and after months of unanswered questions and uncertainties, I was wondering what I could do, if anything, to resolve the dilemma.

The room at that early morning hour was luminous as the moonlight shone in through the window. I sat up and casually looked to the left, and on my wall appeared a large cross. The vision was beautiful, and I wondered, *Is God trying to tell me something?*

In all the years we've lived here, I have never seen such a vision, so I looked closer and saw that it was the moonlight's radiance that beamed through the windowpane, creating the image of a large cross on my wall. As mysterious as this sounds, it even looked as though a silhouette was on the cross.

I reached for the pen and paper on my nightstand as I felt the Lord speak to my heart. And I wrote these words: "Catherine, how can you say I am not in control of this problem? I will lead you to where I want you to be." And then, "I love you."

With those reassuring thoughts, I rested easy and went back to sleep.

The next day, I kept thinking about that vision of the large cross on my wall. I couldn't get it off my mind as I prayed, "Thank You, Lord, for giving me great hope and comfort." Again I was reminded that if we have the Lord on our side, what else do we need?

To overcome our challenges, we must talk with God daily, obey His Word, and His grace will sustain us. Let us take His glorious promises into our hearts as we recall Psalm 18:35: "You have also given me the shield of Your salvation; Your right hand has held me up, Your gentleness has made me great" (Psalm 18:35 NKJV).

THROUGH ADVERSITY WE BECOME STRONGER

Sophia and I went for a walk this lovely spring morning. Everywhere we looked, we saw the trees unfurling green leaves, the dew sparkling on the grass, and blossoming flowers glowing like radiant jewels under the morning sun-filled sky. Squirrels were leaping and tiny chipmunks hid from sight in heaps of rocks as we listened to the festive songs of the birds.

Three-year-old Sophia bent down and looked in wonder at some pink, yellow, and purple crocuses peeking through the recently thawed soil. I knelt down and met her wide blue eyes. They were shining as she said, "Mommy, God made this flower."

I hugged her and agreed, "Yes, Sophia, this flower is a sign of hope. God kept it safe and warm, even through the cold winter." Sophia nodded and smiled, skipping along as we continued our walk.

The soft winds refreshed my spirit and we walked a little farther, down a long, winding road full of twists and turns, past a running stream where all of nature's sounds were blended in perfect harmony. Then a thought came to my mind: *God does not always take us the easiest way.*

I smiled as, at that moment, I saw a humble little caterpillar inching its way up a tree branch. "Look, Sophia," I said. "That caterpillar will soon be transformed into a lovely, colorful butterfly." Sophia giggled and watched the creature's progress up the tree.

The caterpillar has always reminded me that out of great struggle and seeming voids, life is renewed and becomes even more beautiful than ever before. Struggles and tribulations, which we all face, in reality carry with them special gifts of love.

The lesson of triumphing over obstacles ultimately brings us something precious. Each challenge we encounter advances us along the pathway God desires, thus transforming us from "glory to glory." Scripture says, "The Lord—who is the Spirit—makes us more and more like him as we are changed into his glorious image" (2 Corinthians 3:18 NLT).

The key to overcoming adversity is to accept, with peace in our hearts, the daily tests we are presented in the form of challenges. Remember, you would not be who you are today without the life experiences you have had, for you grow in character, learn, and develop in the challenging times. Are you in the middle of a storm right now? Look up, beyond the clouds, to the sky the good Lord spread above you—a precious canopy of pure blue to remind you to have patience in times of trouble.

I like the advice of the famed Canadian physician Sir William Osler, who said, "Draw a circle around one twenty-four-hour period of time and don't bother your mind with worries about what you need to accomplish outside of that." By having hope and trusting that God will clear your path, you will see that the clouds are temporary and the sun will shine within your heart once again.

On our first date, Todd and I went for a ride on his cruiser. Since I hadn't really been on a boat before, I called a childhood friend of mine ahead of time who knew about boating. "Dave, on Sunday, I am going on a boat ride with a date. What do I do on a boat?"

He said, "Catherine, just sit there."

Sometimes, when uncertainties are all around us, that is what we need to do: just sit there, and wait for the deliverance of the Lord. Even though things seem out of control, despite impossible odds God is in control and is never overruled. So, come back to a place of peace.

Accordingly, today, take your eyes off your worries and frustrations; fix your gaze far above them, all the way up to heaven, where there is perfect peace. We can go through adversity and become embittered, or we can overcome those feelings and move ahead into the joyous light of God's love.

I am reminded of a story by an unknown author that a teacher friend, Kitty, sent to me. In the narrative, a king offered a prize to the artist who could best paint a picture of peace. Many artists submitted their work, and from them the king selected two pictures he was quite fond of. "I shall choose between these," the king announced.

In the first scene was a calm, undisturbed lake surrounded by tall, serene mountains. Overhead was a tranquil blue sky with beautiful puffy, white clouds. It looked like the perfect representation of peace.

The second picture had mountains in it as well. But these mountains were rugged and harsh. Above the mountains was a murky, dark sky filled with rain that beat down on all below. Stark lightning bolts streaked through the sky. The depiction did not seem peaceful at all.

But when the king stared more closely at the picture, he saw a tiny green bush at the side of the dark mountain. Inside the bush the artist had portrayed a mother bird building her nest, sheltered from the raging storm around her.

The king unhesitatingly selected the second picture as the winner.

"Why?" you may ask.

The king explained his reasoning: "Peace does not have to be where there is no noise, confusion, or trouble. The real meaning of peace is existing in the midst of turmoil and still holding hope and contentment in your heart."

Remain in peace, hope, and harmony, and hear all around you the birds' sweet songs.

At this moment, God is bringing all things together for your highest good.

GOD, I WILL LEAVE THIS UP TO YOU

Why am I having these problems?" "Why am I facing terrible opposition?" "Why are things not going my way?"

Did you ever consider that the reason "bad" things happen isn't because of what you did or didn't do? Nor is the reason necessarily where you've been or where you are today. Maybe it's because of where you're going!

Very often, when you are drawing near to realizing your God-inspired destiny, you will have to confront unexpected difficulties.

A question I am often asked is, "How do I know where God wants me?" One of the keys I have learned in my life is that when God wants you somewhere, there will be no doubt as to where He wants you to be. Pay attention to His leading, to His signs, to your heart's desire. And hold on to hope as you wait on the Lord.

It took many years for God to test my faith and teach me to wait patiently for His answer regarding the direction He wanted for my career. And in just thirty minutes one evening, I received it.

Let me explain. This past Saturday night, I was watching a church service on television. The minister spoke on the subject "A Better Way to Live." *Wow*, I thought, *that title sounds familiar.*

Then I recalled that many years ago, my favorite author, Og Mandino, wrote a book bearing that same title.

I don't know why, but I walked into my home office, searched the hundreds of titles on my bookshelves, and found the small, burgundy-colored paperback. Yes, the title was *A Better Way to Live*, and it had been years since I read this beloved book. The pages were yellowed, tattered, and worn, but remembering its timeless wisdom and the great impact it had on my life, I thought I would take a look at Mandino's book again before bedtime.

I want to share with you a little about the effect that Og Mandino's words have had on my life. There were many times, in the years following my mother's untimely death, that I wanted to die. Confused, depressed, and alone, I would think of all the ways I could take my life.

My first connection with Og Mandino's work came through a casual acquaintance, a photographer. About twenty years ago, this photographer shared with me another of Mandino's books titled *The Greatest Salesman in the World*. I loved the book and raced to the library to find more of his books. His personal account of how he triumphed over his own mounting obstacles and achieved personal and professional success strongly affected me. With every gentle word of wisdom I read, I felt myself being dragged out of the depths of hopelessness and despair.

Now, dear readers, back to my Saturday night story: about thirty minutes later on that warm evening, I walked upstairs and kissed my younger girls good night. Todd was sitting in a rocking chair in the playroom, reading a storybook to Sophia, so I went into my bedroom, comfortably adjusted my pillow, sat on the bed, leaned back, and started reading, once again, Mandino's *A Better Way to Live.*

I flipped to the first chapter, where he described how he came up with the title for the book. On the next page he spoke of "fate, chance, luck, coincidence"—where God intervenes and resolves problems.

I turned to the next page and then stared in amazement at what I saw. In the sentence on top of page six, Mandino wrote, ". . . on my way home to phone my Bantam editor, Michelle Rapkin."

I read it yet again, barely trusting what my eyes were conveying to me: "Michelle Rapkin."

I sat staring at the name . . . *No, it couldn't be. My Michelle?* I asked myself wonderingly, my heart catching. *My own editor, Michelle, who had bought my own book, was Mandino's editor twenty years ago?!*

Three months earlier, following too many coincidences to ignore, I signed on with the wonderful people at Hachette to publish this book, thanks to the enthusiasm of the acquiring editor, Michelle Rapkin.

Immediately I called my agent and dear friend, Claire, and told her what happened. "I have goose bumps!" Claire exclaimed.

Life has come around full circle.

Twenty years ago, my favorite author, Og Mandino, and his editor, Michelle, unknowingly saved my life. And now, knowing the importance of passing on words of inspiration, I am so grateful to become my own readers' voice of hope and encouragement.

As long as I live, I will never forget this experience. After countless years of wondering where my path would lead me, after sacrifice and suffering, this was God's answer to my prayer, my sign, and my miracle.

This book that you hold in your hands was indeed meant to be.

Dear readers, know that no situation can hold you back as long as you believe in the power of hope. When the road you are traveling twists and turns, remember that God is keeping step with you, and His presence will be your safety and your defense. Thus, begin each morning as I do, with His Word firmly planted in your mind recalling, "He is my refuge and my fortress, my God, in whom I trust" (Psalm 91:2 NIV).

HOPE: Key to Your Heart's Desire

○━ᴋ With hope in your heart, you can rise above the storm to where your flight is calm and peaceful. Remember, life is full of risks to be taken, so move forward, find undiscovered possibilities, seize them, and pursue them enthusiastically.

○━ᴋ Most people who achieve the extraordinary get off to a slow and difficult start. But they are victorious because they hold on to hope and refuse to yield to discouragement. Take one step at a time, and before you know it, you'll have reached your goal.

○━ᴋ I like to recall the proverb "Hope holds the head up." I interpret this to mean that hope sees the unseen, believes the intangible, and accomplishes the impossible.

○━ᴋ God does miraculous things for us, not because we are perfect, but because we have hope and believe in Him. Watch as He puts the pieces of your life together in a way that will exceed your greatest expectations.

○—🔑 Focus on doing the right thing, even if you're tempted to take the easy way out. Keep your eyes on a life of spiritual excellence. When you focus on the highest, good things will happen to you.

○—🔑 Don't mope; keep trying. Hope is most powerful when backed up by action. If you can't go around the problem, go over it or under it, or even right through it, and straight on to success.

○—🔑 As you travel the road of life, use your experiences to encourage others around you who may be struggling. Do all you can to help them climb their mountains, for the real joy in life comes from reaching out to help others and holding up a mirror to their well-earned successes and their unlimited potential.

Key #5:
GRATITUDE

Be filled with the Spirit; speaking to yourselves in
psalms and hymns and spiritual songs, singing and
making melody in your heart to the Lord; giving
thanks always for all things unto God and the
Father in the name of our Lord Jesus Christ.

(Ephesians 5:18–20 KJV)

There's a very dear man I have known for many years now. He is a delightful gentleman in his late eighties, and I found out, quite by coincidence, that back in the 1930s he actually grew up with my mother!

Since we first met over fifteen years ago, Raymond has been like a father to me, and I know he feels I'm as close to a daughter as he could find. I truly love this man.

Although Raymond is legally blind, needs a hearing aid, and has many challenges to overcome, you would never know it, for he never complains. Regardless of his age, he has continued to live life to the fullest, for his years on earth only make him more grateful for his ability to still be here, sharing his wisdom with others.

Once I asked him his secret for staying in such a state of joy, and he affirmed, "I thank the Lord each morning for what He has given to me."

A grateful heart always becomes a happy heart. And from our appreciation and love of God, we can grow a beautiful harvest.

I've heard it said that the Lord has two dwelling places, one in heaven and the other in a thankful heart. So let us "give thanks to the LORD! . . . Sing to Him; sing psalms to Him; talk of all His wondrous works!" (1 Chronicles 16:8–9 NKJV).

Remember, the Lord so loves us that He brought us here to live in a world of endless opportunities, beneath His cornucopia of blessings. And for that, let us rejoice, give thanks, and offer up our hearts in gratitude.

GIVE THANKS FOR THE LITTLE THINGS

One crisp fall evening, I recall sitting on the burgundy love seat in our family room with our then-five-year-old Gabriella beside me. Todd made a fire in the fireplace, and we moved closer to the hearth to feel the warmth of the newly lit flame. As I gently touched Gabriella's long, dark curly hair, she hummed a song of thankfulness.

We began toasting marshmallows and I sang along with my daughter. And at that particular instant, happy and fulfilled, with my loving family close by, I realized how precious every single moment of our lives can be.

These past few years have brought with them their share of challenges, but I often ponder, *Do the difficulties we face draw us closer to the One who said, "Give thanks in all things"?*

"But Catherine," you might say, "how can we give thanks when the challenges of life rise up before us? And why does God let us go through such trials?"

Those are all good questions. I have come to believe that when God puts these things in His divine order, they always work together for good. We have to believe that even our trials eventually will create something wonderful. Trials can provide us with our greatest triumphs. When we have the right attitude, challenges often propel us toward success, like jet fuel shooting a rocket faster and faster toward its unseen destination.

A recent letter reminded me of this. A reader wrote that when their son had a catastrophic illness, she and her husband went into financial ruin, losing everything, including their family business. But miraculously, with only a 15 percent chance of survival, their son won his battle for life, awakening within them a new surge of gratitude to God.

Throughout the tests and the trials, they continued to glorify God, and in spite of a wave of financial hardships, they have seen His hand in many blessings. Today they celebrate good health and loving relationships, and a powerful relationship with a God who never fails.

What is the key to thriving despite hardship? When we choose to be thankful and bless the Lord in the midst of our difficulties, we are opening ourselves to let Him move mightily in our lives. Even when we don't understand *why*, we must rest, thank God, and trust in His faithfulness for the outcome.

One of my favorite quotes is from the eighteenth-century minister William Law. He wrote, "If anyone could tell you the shortest, surest way to all happiness and perfection he must tell you to make it a rule to yourself to thank and praise God for everything that happens to you. For it is certain that whatever seeming calamity happens to you, if you thank and praise God for it, you turn it into a blessing."

God is holding us in His mighty hand and loves us with all His heart. And as we glorify Him, miracles occur. We are told in the Scriptures to "enter into His gates with thanksgiving, and into His courts with praise" (Psalm 100:4 NKJV). As we give thanks, recalling His many gifts to us throughout our lives, and rejoice in the abundance of God's tender mercies, our hearts and spirits grow warm and contented.

Today I am asking you to ponder all the wonders that God has created for you, keeping in mind what matters most:

your relationship with the Creator, your beloved family, true friends, good health, your home, your freedom, this great country, kindly deeds, unique talents, unexpected acts of thoughtfulness, nature's peace, darling pets, and your work and contributions.

Every life is a privilege, a cherished gift. Live yours to the fullest, seize it, and embrace every moment as a miracle. Joy does not simply happen to us. We have to choose joy and keep on choosing it every single day, giving thanks for the blessings we have and sincerely sharing our gifts with others.

One day, I was at a local gift shop that carried my Grace Line dinner plates. A teacher from my daughter's school was looking around the store and told me how much she liked my dishes. "Catherine, your idea is a wonderful reminder for all of us to give thanks at mealtime."

Grateful for her kind words, I replied, "I am so glad you like them!"

The woman went on to say that she thought the plates would be a great gift for her sister. "My sister has been going through many trials and difficulties," she declared, "and maybe saying the graces on these plates and focusing on gratitude will help her overcome her present situation."

Then, pausing for a moment, she looked down and said, "Unfortunately, I can't afford to buy the plates for her at this time."

After talking for a few more moments, we said our good-byes and soon afterward I left the gift shop.

I drove home, made dinner for the family, and returned a few e-mails, but all night, I kept recalling our conversation. I just couldn't stop my mind from drifting back, recalling the many times I was so destitute that I had to do without. I'd even had to sell the few pieces of jewelry I possessed in order to pay my rent.

But one thing I always resolved to do, regardless of my circumstances, was to say a prayer of thankfulness. I was constantly trying to stay positive and focus on my blessings, for I believed that a grateful heart could alter everything.

During those challenging days of the past—and even today—I donned "a garment of praise" expressing gratitude to God for what was good and right in my life (Isaiah 61:3 NIV). Change did not happen in my life overnight, but little by little, a transformation took place.

The day after I had met the teacher in the gift shop, I drove to our warehouse, cheerfully picked up two boxes of Grace Line plates, went to the school, and dropped them off in secret. One set was for the teacher and another set for her sister. I guess the teacher figured out that the presents came from me, because a beautiful card came in the mail. She had nearly despaired of people's ability to be kind, she said. With something as simple as a surprise gift, her faith was restored.

A reader contributed a special quote from Benjamin Franklin: "A man's story is not told solely by a list of his grand accomplishments, but rather by his smaller, daily goods." The things that count the most should never be at the mercy of things that mean the least. Let us choose to share moments of kindness with others, help when we can, show our gratitude, and see beauty everywhere. For God writes His words to us on the faces of babies, on the hands of the elderly, on petals of roses, and in the shimmering stars above.

I often think of our dear friends John and Ruth. Whenever I spend time with them, I come home feeling like a better, more joyful human being, thanks to their kindheartedness, faithfulness, and fine example. They follow a wonderful philosophy of life: "Let no one come into contact with us without leaving a happier, better, and more thankful person." The more time I spend with this wonderful couple, the more convinced I am that this is what I want, too.

Love is the beauty we take with us wherever we go. And I am so grateful for the love that we share, dear readers, for the memories and the blessings that are given to me through your heartwarming letters.

Back in my family room that delightful fall evening, my precious Gabriella hugged me and said, "I love you, Mama." Kissing her forehead, I held her close and felt tears slipping down my cheeks. Embracing her gently, I sang a prayer of gratitude to God.

THANK GOD AGAIN AND AGAIN FOR HIS BLESSINGS

I do it often. I make a list of the good things that God has done for me, and then one by one I thank Him for His countless gifts. Thinking back and reminding myself of my blessings builds up my faith and brings me hope and strength.

Let's try this experiment together. Take a piece of paper and attach it to your refrigerator or bathroom mirror. Or put it by your bedside or on your desk at work. Each day, add one thing for which you are truly thankful. Then share your gratitude with God by listing them all, one by one, in prayers of thanksgiving. In the midst of difficulties or tribulations, as you look back at your gratitude list you'll find that golden glow on life once again restored to you.

I'm reminded of a story I heard long ago about a missionary who was held hostage in another country under terrible conditions. In his first interview after his release, he was asked how he coped with despair. The missionary responded, "I recalled my blessings."

"Blessings?" the reporter questioned.

"Yes," he replied. "I remembered the love of my family; I reminisced about the birth of my children; I called to mind an encouraging letter I received; I recalled how God had delivered me, loved me, and supplied my needs in the past. And I prayed, thanking God constantly for the grace and mercies He had always bestowed on me."

The missionary explained that as he praised and worshiped God, he felt himself being lifted above his difficulties. Prayer and praise are very powerful; they help us overlook our present obstacles and call our attention to gratitude. Then, magically, solutions to our problems begin to appear.

Here's another successful key to getting through rough times: thank God for the good things that are on the way. If you are sick, offer thanks to God for the healing that is on its way. If you've experienced a setback, say, "Thank You, God. I know You have something better for me in the days to come." Express gratitude to God as if He has already brought your dreams to pass. And as you express your belief and gratitude to your Creator, He will respond in miraculous ways.

Do you remember when your strength was renewed, your loved one healed, or your child delivered from an unhappy situation? Do you recall when just the right person was put in your path, or when you were offered that scholarship, dream job, or long-desired opportunity? Can you bring to mind when you were held back from making a mistake, your needs were met, or a way was shown when it seemed as though there was no way?

Think back to when you were in a situation you thought would never work out, and then, amazingly, everything fell into place. How about when you were at the right place at the right time and received an unexpected blessing? As Scripture tells us, "Give thanks to the LORD, for his steadfast love endures for ever" (2 Chronicles 20:21 RSV).

I give thanks every day to the Lord for what He has done for me. As a young woman, I was ready to give up after finding my mother dead; I thought constantly of ways I might take my own life. But God gave me His Word and encouraged me to carry on.

When I doubted, He provided me with hope, telling me and then showing me that He had plans for me.

When I lived alone for years in an unsafe neighborhood, God shielded and protected me.

And just when I thought my situation would never turn around, someone gave me a chance. And with that opportunity, I was able to share the words and wisdom I had been given with others who needed exactly that.

When I wondered if I'd ever meet the right person to love and who would love me, and when others told me discouragingly, "Catherine, your biological clock is ticking," He sent me my soul mate.

Then, after the complicated birth of our third daughter, Sophia, when I could barely lift my head off the pillow, He sent me His strength and restored my health.

When I needed words of encouragement to bring me out of a descent into the depths of despair, He sent me angels in the form of true friends. For years, when I was being unfairly treated in business, I carried on in faith. And now God has showered me with blessings beyond measure that have replaced my losses, pain, and frustrations.

Yes, my personal gratitude list goes on and on. And when I speculated if I'd ever find a vocation I loved and would be of service to others, He led me to each one of you.

NATURE'S BEAUTY FILLS US WITH GRATITUDE

Look outdoors to receive God's gifts of nature, which bring so much peace and tranquility. When you get in touch with God's creation, it will transform your life.

I think of the vibrant pink roses growing so beautifully in the front of our home. The rains come, along with the wind and the cold nights, and still the roses bloom with a brightness and beauty that surpass fine art and stately architecture.

These are magnificent symbols of hope, peace, and the mind of God. His vibrant blossoms bring forth our adoration of a higher level of life that far surpasses any man-made scientific achievements.

God knows that, as little children, we imitate what we see. What did He put before us? Gazing outdoors, I see the trees in the woods with branches uplifted in praise of their Maker. These remind us to be thankful and full of praise to God for all that we have. Why do we give glory and thanks to the Lord? Because when we praise Him, we are filled with His joy and sweetness. Scripture says, "Rejoice in the Lord always. Again I will say, rejoice!" (Philippians 4:4 NKJV).

The endless blue sky, in all its wonder, has no limit. Similarly, your highest goals are limitless because they are inspired by God.

Far out in the ocean, I see small birds, perfectly secure, riding on the highest and roughest waves. The birds are not fearful because they sense their Creator. Let's call to mind the Scripture "Do not worry about your life, what you will eat or what you will drink; nor about your body, what you will put on. . . . Your heavenly Father knows that you need all these things" (Matthew 6:25, 32 NKJV).

The Bible says, "Take a lesson from the ants" (Proverbs 6:6 TLB). These tiny creatures know how important it is to stay busy because if they do not work, they do not eat. Therefore, we must work together in harmony to achieve the perfect goal of supplying others and ourselves.

The lowly caterpillar transformed into a lovely butterfly reminds us that those who believe often emerge from great struggles renewed and seeing life as even more beautiful than before.

Artist Claude Monet once said, "I paint as a bird sings." The bird's dazzling notes undoubtedly inspired him, for he painted blades of grass with the sparkle of dew and produced colors that glittered in the sunlight.

A reader wrote that when hard times come, she stays alert to God's voice and love. They are always there, she says, and He is working out his purposes in every circumstance.

I hear the murmur of the wind's whisper, and I see the refreshingly clean sweep that it makes, just as the Holy Spirit sweeps clean our souls. God knows we were born to experience the earth as He meant it to be: a completely pure place, a home planet of beauty, where love and thankfulness are felt and shown. Here, one day "the wolf . . . shall dwell with the lamb, the leopard shall lie down with the young goat, the calf and the young lion and the fatling together" (Isaiah 11:6 NKJV).

The Word of God is a seed, and when watered with praise and thanksgiving it blossoms in our hearts with glorious rainbow colors. A rainbow is a symbol of God's promises—promises that always come to pass. We must simply wait with the patience of a stately tree, our arms reaching upward in thanksgiving and praise.

BE THANKFUL: GOD ACCEPTS US FOR WHO WE ARE

Like most people at one time or another, I have struggled to feel accepted.

I recall one of my grade-school teachers instructing the group to line up before beginning our gym class. He would then choose two students, and those children would pick the ones they wanted to be on their sports teams.

Because I was so uncoordinated in sports, I was always one of the last to be selected. Disheartened, I would go home after school and ask my mother, "Why am I always last?"

In her soft, consoling voice, she would hug me and then say, "Catherine, remember this: the last will be first."

As a child, I did not realize that this was a verse from the Bible. Today, I find myself saying that to my own children. In God's family, "the last will be first" (Matthew 20:16 NKJV).

No matter what others may say or think, remember: you mean more to Him than His own life. God made you as you are and loves you as you are, and there are no conditions on His love.

Furthermore, any rejection you have felt has had no effect on His love and acceptance of you; His love for all His children is pure and strong and unswerving.

So be grateful for you!

Some businesses, strangely enough, follow the military strategy of breaking their employees down to then "rebuild them" as they would like. Associates may make fun of you, gossip, and retaliate. Even family members may criticize and manipulate you, while supposed friends may gain your trust only to betray you later.

How do you survive the hurt, the humiliation, the intense pain? Let me share my own experience with you.

Years ago, my place of employment underwent yet another staff change. I was used to such changes, so I went about my work as usual. But a new employee seemed to criticize and ridicule everything I did. One day, after speaking with this person, I found myself on the verge of tears. I was shaking, unable to focus on the work that sat on my desk. Other coworkers were unfailingly kind and supportive and urged me not to give up. Their words gave me the strength to carry on and to continue treating this person with kindness and respect. Within the year, though, another staff change relieved us of the difficult employee.

This experience ended up teaching me many valuable lessons: the lesson of "Do to others what you would have them do to you" (Matthew 7:12 NIV), the lesson of standing firm, and the lesson that "love never fails" (1 Corinthians 13:8 NKJV). Most important was the lesson of keeping the faith, because I knew within me that God would find a way for me to overcome this situation.

I know a good, kindhearted teenager who, while growing up, was rejected and belittled by his father. Although he began his life with optimism, he eventually started keeping company with the wrong crowd, became addicted to drugs, and spent many years in jail. He lost faith in a loving God and sought approval from other lost souls. I have received countless letters from those within the barren walls of prisons; most admit that the unfavorable influences of others were the cause of their decline.

There's an old expression: tell me who you choose as friends, and I'll tell you who you are. Bad company, unfortunately, can corrupt good character. No matter how strong you are, polluters of your soul can ruin your life and prevent you from becoming all you can be.

The wrong friends can certainly lead to unexpected troubles. I received an unforgettable letter from a young woman confirming this: "I am serving a sentence on a drunken driving case," she wrote. "I hit another car and the passenger died. I have never been in trouble, came from a wonderful family, and had a beautiful life. Please tell your readers to protect themselves from unhealthy influences—it can truly mean the difference between life and death."

Leave the places where you are being tempted. Guard your precious life. Don't let impostors tear up your dreams. Your associations are so very important. Know this: people often reveal who they really are when they meet you for the first time. Whatever they show you . . . *believe it!*

Life is not easy, so we all must practice unwavering communication with God. This will build our confidence and hone our abilities to keep balance and know we are deeply loved. It is then that we can overcome difficulties by recognizing the truth.

Now, let me ask you this: do you like yourself? Don't worry

about what other people say or do; it is your opinion of yourself that matters most.

Next, take yourself up a few notches. I am not recommending conceit or vanity. But confidence and self-esteem must be cultivated. What we plant in our gardens will come up. What we absorb within our minds will grow. Proverbs 23:7 reminds us that as we think, we are. . . .

I smile when I think about what Gabriella just told me. Apparently, her second-grade teacher asked the students to pick two outstanding people in the class for an award she would be presenting at the end of the school year. I asked Gabriella whom she picked.

Radiating self-assurance she confidently declared, "Me and Juliana."

"Why?"

"Because Juliana is brave . . . and I am kind." And I agreed on both counts.

Today, make a list of ten great things about you. Remember all the good that others have said about you. Toss aside any negative words or thoughts; they're not important.

In fact, will you allow me to start your list?

1. Faith in God
2. Share encouragement
3. The ability to smooth out life's problems
4. A giving heart
5. An attitude of gratitude

With qualities like these, you will be able to get through anything!

Boost your self-confidence by realizing that our omnipotent God has a purpose that you alone can fulfill: it's your destiny alone, no one else's. If the least bit of discouragement creeps in, stop it in its tracks. Avoid catastrophic thinking. If something difficult happens to you, try treating your situation as a challenge rather than a disaster. Set your sights and thoughts on things that are supportive and encouraging. Consider nothing else, for negatives are not of God.

Promptly challenge yourself to shed unhealthy habits. Get enough rest, eat healthful foods, spend quiet time in prayer every day, exercise, have creative outlets while dieting (always checking with your doctor before starting a diet or exercise regimen). Henry David Thoreau said, "Every man is the builder of a temple, called his body."

God puts seeds of Himself in our hearts, but they work only if we believe. I know the Bible says, "My sheep recognize my voice" (John 10:27 TLB). For that reason, when I hear the truth, something inside me says, "Yes. I hear it and I give thanks for it!"

SEE THE GOOD AND LIVE A LIFE OF GRATITUDE

Tell me something good that happened today," I said to Lauren and Gabriella after they climbed down from the school bus.

Sometimes I ask in a different way, as in, "Who did a kind deed?" or "Who has something to be grateful for?" However I word it, the question always means the same thing. It is a call for rejoicing and focusing on what's good and what's right in their lives.

Every day is a gift from God. So let's get up in the morning with joy, enthusiasm, and thankfulness. Let's look for the beauty in each day, search for the good, and rejoice in the finest.

Some time ago, a friend of mine told me that when her dad comes home from work, the first thing he says is "All right, what happened today?" as if he expects the worst. Worn down from his negative thinking, my friend asked, "Catherine, do you have any thoughts that I can pass on to my father?"

I suggested that she ask her father to try this approach: when he arrives home from work the first question he should ask is, "What *good* happened today?" "Be sure he always looks for the *good*," I said. "Then have him thank God for His faithfulness and ask your dad to say aloud how he wants his life and his family members' lives to be."

I love to recall this Scripture: "You will . . . declare a thing, and it will be established for you" (Job 22:28 NKJV). Like attracts like; good produces good. And joy generates more joy. So, be determined to center your thoughts on the goodness and loveliness of life, and speak aloud the things you desire.

Last week we were celebrating Sophia's third birthday at a local restaurant, and my friend's father was there having dinner. It was wonderful meeting him. I felt as though I had known him for years as he took my hand and said, "Catherine, just that small adjustment in my outlook has made all the difference. Now, I look for the good." And more and more, he finds it.

The key? Choice! Will you choose to expect, speak of, and focus on good things or bad?

Remember, the decisions of the mind are very private, but the whole world sees the results.

Our thoughts do play a major role in our lives. I know from experience that amazing things transpire when we look for the good with thankfulness, because an optimistic, pleasant, and appreciative mind-set will lead us toward happy, healthy, and abundant living.

I think about Todd and his amazing talents and abilities. He seems to know how to do everything well. Whether it's fulfilling a client's demands for automation technology, constructing a forty-foot deck, patiently brushing out our daughters' long hair, graciously assisting a friend or neighbor with electrical work, problem-solving our home computer's latest challenge, shopping for last-minute dinner ingredients, volunteering at our daughter's school, mowing the lawn on a hot summer day, or helping me bring one of my many ideas to fruition—he carries out every responsibility with confidence and assurance.

And no matter the task, he does it with an attitude of thankfulness. Calm, contented, good-natured, and always accommodating and appreciative, Todd has a most remarkable personality.

A willing, grateful, agreeable outlook is a treasure from God. It makes everything in life peaceful. Think about it—doesn't your attitude color your day?

"Catherine," I've been asked, "how can a thankful, optimistic attitude become a dominant factor in my life?" It must be practiced. We should never lose the wonder of what God has done for us. We each have experienced wonderful occurrences that seem impossible to explain. That's why we must never lose sight of His tiniest miracle. In order to attract more of the blessings that life has to offer, we must appreciate what we already have.

A business colleague told me that when he feels a bit down he gets a piece of paper, draws a line down the middle, and writes on one side all the things that are right with his life, his accomplishments and dreams. Then, on the other side of the paper, he lists all the things that are wrong. He said that after he looks at all his assets, he has a much more positive perspective!

Every day when I ask my girls to share with me their good deeds, good news, or gratitude, I receive so many positive responses that the answers have been a profound influence on my daughters, Todd, and myself.

"Mom, I did a good deed today at school," declared Gabriella as she ran to me when I picked her up from softball practice.

"What did you do, honey?" I asked.

"I helped Emily to the nurse, because she fell on the field," she stated.

Another day, when we were driving to the post office, Gabriella said from the backseat of the car, "Mommy, guess what good I did today."

"Tell me," I urged, marveling at her continuing list of good deeds.

"I gave my apple to Courtney because she did not have a snack. I am so grateful for a friend like her!" she exclaimed.

One afternoon, Lauren came home from school, and I had her favorite snack, a dish of warm macaroni and cheese, ready for her at the table. She took a mouthful and uttered, "I'm thankful, Mommy . . . for you!"

Hugging her, I laughed, saying, "And I am thankful for you!"

Together, we have learned to look for the good in the commonplace. And my girls have increased their awareness of all the goodness, beauty, and miracles around us and thank God for them.

I'm reminded that the way to a joy-filled life is in these words:

"Once and only once I pass; if a good deed I may do, if a kindness I may show to a suffering fellow man, let me do it while I can. Let me not defer nor neglect it, for it is plain I shall not pass this way again."

SIMPLIFIED LIVING BRINGS JOY TO OUR LIVES

The secret of happiness lies in our ability to extract happiness from common things. True power comes from simple acts of life. Our faith is built on routine, daily practices, and ordinary occurrences.

God is like this, for He hides Himself in simplicity. Every gorgeous sunrise, scarlet sunset, and the diamond-studded sky we witness in this world of ours at night is an imprint of our Creator.

The truth of the matter is that I love my day-to-day existence, ordinary days, casual occasions, and my usual routine.

For our ninth wedding anniversary, Todd and I went out for a quiet dinner for two, which is a rare occurrence. Our reservations were at six in the evening, and by seven we were finished with our meal. We strolled past some charming stores in town and window-shopped.

The country air was pure and sweet, and the beautiful scenery acted as a healing balm over us after long, busy days. Lingering in the enchanting moment, we smiled at each other and expressed how thankful we were for our many blessings.

Just then I realized that the down-to-earth, uncomplicated way we live our lives teaches us who we are. We need not spend our time and money on expensive and outlandish things; for us, the clean, easy, calm, and peaceful life is the way we prefer to spend our days.

One day, two friends, Lori and Joanna, were talking. "How is it that you are always so calm and content?" Lori asked. "You never seem to get depressed."

With smiling eyes, Joanna said, "I know the secret."

"What secret is that?" Lori eagerly questioned.

"I'll tell you all about it, but you have to promise to share the secret with others."

"I will," Lori assured.

"The secret is this: I have learned there is little I can do in my life that will make me truly happy. Therefore, I must depend on God for my joy and have faith in Him to meet my desires."

Joanna continued. "When a need arises, I thank God and trust that He is supplying my need according to His glory and riches. Most of the time, I don't require half of what I think I do. God has never let me down before. And since I learned this secret, I am truly contented, thankful, and blessed."

Lori's first thought was, *How could that be . . . ?* But reflecting on her own life, she recalled how she believed a spiffy new car would make her happy. But it didn't. She thought a better-paying job would make her secure, but it hadn't. Did that expensive vacation bring her joy? Not really.

Then she thought about her greatest delight: the wonderful times she spent with her loving husband, holding her newborn grandbabies, her prayer group, the animals she cared for, laughter in her home, family mealtimes, walking in the countryside, her charity work, and sharing the bounty of her garden. These simple, priceless moments were truly gifts from God.

We can't depend on things to make us happy. Only God in His infinite wisdom can do that. Let us pray for God's grace and His peace, and surely, He will give them to us.

People like Joanna, who have real joy in their hearts, know how to savor the simple things that lighten heavier days. They are not unnerved by events and difficulties; instead, they concentrate on pleasantness that will erase the unpleasant. They uncover life's sweet possibilities to get more delight out of each day.

I once heard about the unique approach that the early Quakers had to getting answers to life's problems. They would sit in perfect silence before the Lord, letting every outward sense become still. Then they'd drop their problem into the great, deep pool of God's knowledge and, in gratitude, serenely wait. Not very long after, they say, the answer became crystal clear.

A lady I know thought she would never smile again when her husband left her with three small children. So she sat in her room in complete silence and asked God for a sense of humor. He gave it to her, and now, thirty-five years later, she has people in her life who appreciate her and her well-brought-up, happy children.

I have heard it said, "Those who live joyfully live lightly." These people use humor as a soothing balm that takes the sharp edges off life. This proverb offers us another key: keep your face toward the sunshine and the shadows will fall behind you.

As a joy-filled, grateful person, you will see the hand of God in everything.

I love the silence in the wee morning hours, when the birds first begin their melodious song and the world begins anew. And I embrace the fresh, pristine day full of wonderful possibilities.

"But Catherine, how can I simplify my life when there is so much complexity in it?" you may ask.

Try this: for the first five, ten, or fifteen minutes of the day, arrange a meeting with our wonderful Creator and say, "Thank

You" for all that He has provided. Throughout the day, continue to express your thanks to Him.

Then delight in the simple pleasures of life: warm conversations between like-minded friends, helping others, the contagious laughter of little ones, a walk in nature, reading a good book, a new hobby, the touch of someone dear, and relaxing with a cup of warm tea.

In the evening, when fatigue sends you to bed, rest with prayers of faith and hope, maintaining an absolute trust in God's love and goodness. For He said, "Do not let your hearts be troubled; believe in God" (John 14:1 NASB).

Day to day, month to month, decade to decade, I discover the simple pleasures, the tranquility, the harmony, and the balance that these "little things" bring to me.

And I believe that is why, when my husband and I left the restaurant early on our anniversary evening, with the sun not yet set, we walked hand in hand, satisfied just to be together and to have three delightful little girls awaiting our return home. A thankful heart is truly a joy-filled heart.

APPRECIATION MAKES LIFE WORTH LIVING

We bloom under praise like flowers in the sun. Like the pure white water lily that stretches out triumphantly from the depths of murky waters into the glorious light of day, we come alive when people tell us how much they appreciate us.

A reader named Joan wrote to tell me how she eagerly read my column each week and took time to think about each one. She then shared those seeds of truth with others who could benefit from them. She said she, too, wants to make a difference in people's lives.

Appreciation for your fellow human beings and little acts of thoughtfulness can make a huge impact. Kindnesses have a way of being returned to you when you give them liberally and joyfully. Someone's appreciation of your sweetness will make your day! Special people who care from the heart are one of God's ways of showing you His love.

"I make it a point to express my love and gratitude to family and friends," says Liz, a photographer in town. "And I try to be nice to one extra person each and every day." Liz's motto is: "If you want to *have* friends, first you have to *be* a friend."

I know a special person who had cards printed up to pass out whenever she lent a helping hand to another. The cards read "You have been helped today. Instead of payment, please pass this blessing on to someone else."

Our little Sophia, at just three years old, is such a confident, self-assured child. She walks with her head high, with pride and belief in herself. I believe that confidence comes because ever since she was born, I have constantly declared, "Sophia, God loves you," "Mommy and Daddy love you," "Your sisters love you," "Everyone loves you," "You are a smart girl," "We are thankful for you!" and "You're the best." She believes us and passes her self-confidence on to others in the form of loving acts.

Someone needs your appreciation and reassurance today. Let's begin now to give the courage, strength, and confidence every person seeks. Each day, sincerely say, "You're appreciated," to someone for a job well done. Say, "I care about you, and I'm here to help," to a friend in distress. And the most important thing we can do is say, "I am praying for you," when it's time to turn inward in prayer.

If you pack a yummy lunch for your spouse, include a sweet letter of appreciation.

Put an "I love you" card in your child's lunch bag or backpack. I have gotten into the habit of jotting down a few words of praise or encouragement such as: "You are a blessing," "You are a great girl," or "I'm grateful for a wonderful daughter like you" on a little yellow sticky note and placing it in Lauren's and Gabriella's school folders.

One day, Gabriella came home from school and said, "Mommy, I gave the note you wrote to me to one of my friends."

I asked, "Why, honey?"

"Well, I noticed that my friend never gets any notes, and I thought she could use mine."

Others have told me they do the same thing. "I attach notes for my wife and daughters to the bathroom mirror," recalls Ray, a business owner. "I make up little poems and sayings, and my wife, Anne, does the same thing for me," he says. "It really makes a difference!"

My mother loved to give greeting cards, and she never missed an opportunity to send a note of gratitude. The day after she died, I recall looking on a shelf in the kitchen and finding four greeting cards, all addressed and ready to mail. My girls take after their grandmother, because as soon as someone does a kind deed for them or gives them a gift, the first thing they reach for is a greeting card or a piece of paper to write a note of thanks.

Here are a few other ideas: In the workplace, leave a small box of candy on a coworker's desk as a token of your appreciation. Surprise your neighbor with a flowering plant. Make that phone call you have been putting off. Say "Thank you" to your mail delivery person with a ziplock bag full of chocolate chip cookies.

One morning I was in line to order coffee at a drive-thru. When I drove up to the window to pay the clerk, she said, "Your coffee was paid for by the person in front of you." I was surprised and grateful for such a spontaneous act of kindness.

It doesn't have to be a grand, expensive gesture. Just a smile will do. I have a friend who said when money was scarce, for special occasions her family gave one another "tickets" that they created themselves. There were coupons to wash the dishes, cook dinner, fold the laundry, or a free car wash. The family loved getting these "promise tickets" and enjoyed cashing them in later.

A former neighbor who now lives in the South told me she had just mowed her lawn in the heat of the morning. When she sat down, exhausted, on her steps, her new neighbor came around the corner and gave her a bag of homegrown, sun-ripened to-matoes, fresh from his garden, her reward for hard work. As he walked away, gratitude filled her heart, and she asked God to bless him the best way He knew how.

When people write to me and say, "I mail your column and share your books with friends and family around the country," I feel that my readers are just like me. They love to comfort and en-courage, too! It makes me feel as if we're all in the same family.

BE GRATEFUL, FOR THERE IS ONLY ONE OF YOU

I wonder what Todd thinks as he looks at our three darling little girls surrounding him at the dinner table. On the surface, their differences are mostly marked by age, but we also see their amazing similarities. But as similar as our daughters look, we are thankful that each girl is unique with individual traits, abilities, and talents.

Think about this incredible fact: in the entire universe, there is no one else exactly like you. You are truly one of a kind, and you can do miraculous things with your life.

Thankfully, God gave each of us unique gifts that would lift up others, making a profound difference in their lives. What are you doing with your exceptional talents? What are you going to do with God's gift to you?

There is so much more for you to do, to see, to experience. You can take a class, learn an interesting skill, a hobby, explore a local landmark, or take advantage of outdoor concerts, museums, or an art gallery. Browse a tag sale, join an exercise class, and develop new friendships.

This year, my girls' dance teacher, Miss Nancy, and I performed a ballet number in the recital. I took dance lessons for fifteen years, but it had been years since I had been onstage. It was fun for both Miss Nancy and me to step out courageously and perform again. And you know what? Now we can't wait for next year's recital!

Each one of our cats has a favorite spot in our house to sleep. The littlest kitten, Sam, sleeps on the right side of our couch in our family room. Our middle cat, Chris, a long-haired orange beauty, sleeps in the center of our bed among the pillows. And Mickey, our large tabby cat, always sleeps on my office chair. When it comes time for me to work in my home office, I literally share my chair with Mickey. Just imagine me sitting on the very edge of the chair, while Mickey lounges comfortably behind me.

Though, like our three cats, I like routine and customary

habits, I also enjoy expanding my horizons, trying different feats, and meeting new people. I am so grateful for the opportunity to be able to do these things, for I know that not everyone can do so.

I love the account in the Bible about a man named Jabez. In 1 Chronicles 4:10, Jabez calls on the Lord, saying, "Oh, that You would bless me indeed and enlarge my border, and that Your hand might be with me, and that You would keep me from harm that it may not pain me!" (1 Chronicles 4:10 NASB). And God granted him what he requested.

Jabez asked for the blessings that God had for him—and God answered his appeal. Now, if Jabez could ask for and know God's abundant blessings, then you and I can, too.

Life is what you make it; therefore, press forward with joy, self-assurance, and gratitude.

GREAT THINGS ARE IN REACH IF WE
STAY IN A POSITION OF PRAISE

Okay, you're about to embark on a new opportunity; your God-inspired aspirations are about to unfold. You're on the verge of meeting someone who will positively impact your future. Or you're on the brink of overcoming a bad habit. . . .

And then, right before you reach a long-awaited victory, your mind gets bombarded with negative, dispiriting thoughts. After that, you become filled with feelings of inadequacy and become so discouraged you want to give up and not take that next very important step. Then you may ask, *What do I do? Where do I turn?*

One of the answers, I believe, is in a conversation I had with

Ruth, a dear friend who is like a mother to me. A few months ago, I called her one morning. I confided in Ruth about an ongoing and troubling situation that I have been facing for years, and she listened carefully to my dilemma.

Then tenderly, she said, "Catherine, *praise the Lord.*"

I paused for a moment, then asked, "What did you say?"

Ruth went on to remind me that in the Bible it says to give thanks *in all things*, so regardless of the difficulties, we must focus on thankfulness and praise the Lord.

"Catherine," Ruth said in her elegant, melodic voice, "the Lord loves you. He hears your prayers, and He's preparing the ground for you. Sometimes it takes time for Him to set the direction."

Knowing exactly what she meant, I replied, "Thank you, Ruth. I really needed to hear those words today."

"You are in our prayers, dear." Ruth repeated, "Just *praise the Lord* no matter what! That's a wonderful answer to all things."

You have a destiny to fulfill, and you were created to make something wonderful of your life. God has given you special gifts and expects you to express yourself with them. So do not surrender or uproot the beautiful dream you have for your future by allowing the negativity of others or circumstances of the past to drag you down. Proceed with faith, unwavering, toward the goal, and . . . *praise the Lord!*

In my own life, I decided to take Ruth's advice and praise the Lord despite conditions out of my control.

I walked around the house saying, "Thank You, Lord, for the blessings that are just ahead." "God, I praise You for turning the tide of the battle," and "Praise the Lord, You are my strength and my shield." And as I praised, I acted as if God had already answered my requests.

One morning as I was folding the clothes, I uttered, "Praise the Lord." I guess I must say it often without realizing it, as Lauren questioned, "Mommy, why do you say that?"

"Because as I praise God, He gives me the strength to do all the things I have to do."

So on and on, I praised. When situations were going right or when things were in an upheaval, I would call out, "Praise the Lord, for He is good," "I praise You, Lord, and believe You are making a way for me." "Praise the Lord for Your mercy and kindness."

And you know what? A change in my attitude occurred almost at once. Each time a disparaging thought would come to mind, I would erase it with praise. Today, let's get our words and thoughts going in the right direction and praise the Lord!

I read in the Bible that when Paul and Silas were beaten and imprisoned, they began to pray and sing praises to God. Within the dark walls of the prison, God gave them boldness and confidence throughout their ordeal. And in the midnight hour, a miraculous deliverance was brought forth. For praise can miraculously allow doors to swing open and cause chains of bondage to fall away (see Acts 16:16–34).

Have you had hard times this year? God tells us we should give thanks for whatever life brings. And as we do so, victories will happen. God may be working out an inner peace that may not always be visible.

Please keep in mind this key point: do not be defeated, even if a situation seems insurmountable. I have found the darker it gets, the closer you are to success, so do not turn back or give up. Pray, employ patience, and as you wait, praise the Lord! When you call, He hears you. And what looks like a setback can turn out to be an abundant blessing.

It never ceases to amaze me what God can do as we praise and trust in Him. God is called "the author and the finisher of our faith" (Hebrews 12:2 NKJV). This means that as you take the next vital step and praise Him for the blessings on the way, He will be there to help you, guide you, and complete what He started.

God is always working, He never sleeps or slumbers. And even though it may be slow going right now, don't concede, because in His precise timing, your aspirations will come to fruition. God's Word is true, and the heavenly hand that holds your destiny is kind.

Your attitude toward whatever situation you face can influence the outcome. Let yours be an attitude of gratitude. And do as the psalmist advises: "Make a joyful noise unto the LORD, all the earth: make a loud noise, and rejoice, and sing praise" (Psalm 98:4 KJV).

WE BOWED OUR HEADS IN PRAYER AND GRATITUDE AND HE LISTENED

When two little girls bow their heads to pray, God listens. That's what I learned when a friend was going into the hospital to have a tumor removed. Our instant reaction was to call upon the Lord. We made a circle, my little girls and I, held hands, and prayed . . . the three of us formed a prayer chain, with God in the center. For we believe "where two or three are gathered together in My name, I am there in the midst of them" (Matthew 18:20 NKJV).

Therefore, we left the situation in God's mighty hands as a profound peace filled me, and I was at rest in His perfect, sovereign will. And that young lady we prayed for is now completely well.

When we believe, God hears us. What we pray for will come to pass according to His will. He can move mountains. He can always make a way for His will to be done. He knows how to use us to help another, as we just make ourselves available to Him.

Throughout our lives, there are countless times when prayers are answered and miracles occur. Extraordinary wonders are taking place every day, though they are not always visible. In a split second we know God is at work, and it is a treasured moment that will be etched in our hearts evermore. Scripture says, "Since we know he hears us when we make our requests, we also know that he will give us what we ask for" (1 John 5:15 NLT).

How do you pray? Converse with God simply, for He draws near when we talk to Him. Don't just say the same words again and again, but have a real conversation with God. He is of great compassion and understanding and brings comfort, hope, and reassurance. He delights to hear your thoughts and requests made with thanksgiving.

Then, let faith picture the situation you are praying for as being resolved, and hold on to the positive image of its answer. If God can say to a raging sea, "Peace, be still!" (Mark 4:39 NKJV) and it obeys Him, He can certainly control and supply every need of ours.

If He can say, "Daughter, your faith has made you well" (Mark 5:34 NKJV), He can definitely forgive all your sins and start you on a brand-new life. A friend of mine, Maria, always says, "If God brings you to it, He will bring you through it."

So always start prayer with gratitude and let your prayers be full of thanksgiving for God's generous heart. Praise Him from whom all blessings flow, and review the treasured blessings in your life. Believe that God will continue to work in unfathomable ways, and delight in His great wisdom.

When my daughters see pictures of Jesus in their children's books, they give big kisses to Him. God is touched by our loving gestures, caring hearts, and attitudes of gratitude that compel us to take time to do something for another. Inner beauty reveals itself in outward acts of compassion and kindness. Accordingly, by praying for others we are inspired *to do* and *be* God's hands, mouth, and feet.

Jeremiah 31:13 states, "I will turn their mourning into joy, I will comfort them, and give them gladness for sorrow" (Jeremiah 31:13 RSV). Therefore, we will continue to pray . . . my little girls and I. Pray and *do*.

GRATITUDE:
Key to Your Heart's Desire

⊶ When you praise God every morning and evening, the flow of His love will be magnified to you because He is so appreciative of your praise. Thanking Him for your blessings should be habitual, automatic. Scripture says, "Stand every morning to thank and praise the LORD" (1 Chronicles 23:30 NKJV).

⊶ You live only once, so use your hours wisely. Each day ask yourself, *What good things am I going to do today?* And as you spread joyfulness, helpfulness, and goodness wherever you go, watch for the miracles!

⊶ A grateful heart always gives happiness. When you focus on all your blessings, you'll have little time to bemoan what you may not have. Thankfulness is guaranteed to chase away the blues! If you resolve to appreciate all you have going for you, you will be able to move forward toward the extraordinary life that God intends for you to have.

o—⚷   The real measure of wealth is how much you appreciate the love of God and His gifts. Honor, integrity, a clear conscience, time with a loving family, and good health are just a few treasures beyond any material gain. Do not take for granted the things for which you should be so thankful.

o—⚷   These eighteen words from Helen Keller can make a great difference in your thinking as they have in mine: "So much has been given to me; I have not time to ponder that which has been denied."

o—⚷   God may take His time to accomplish what He wants to do in your life, but He has promised to walk with you through everything. So have an attitude of gratitude and trust, with joyful expectation. Situations may look impossible, but with God all things are possible. So be grateful for the bountiful gifts He has given you and make the most of them.

o—⚷   Be a peacemaker and pray for those who come across your path. And as you give with sincere appreciation and praise, and as you watch those around you blossom with success, you will be transformed into the person God created you to be, like Him, always bringing out the best in others.

Key #6:
LOVE

Love . . . bears all things, believes all things,
hopes all things, endures all things. . . .
And now abide faith, hope, love, these three;
but the greatest of these is love.

(1 Corinthians 13:4, 7, 13 NKJV)

How do you want to be remembered? What can you do to leave your mark on this world? I believe it all starts with love.

True love is eternal. Neither time, nor age, nor circumstances can diminish genuine feelings of love. The Bible says, "Many waters cannot quench love, nor can the floods drown it" (Song of Solomon 8:7 NKJV).

Love is the greatest gift in the world, and we all possess the capacity to feel it, to receive it, and to share it with others. To be loved and to give love are the greatest sources of happiness, whether we're rich or poor. With love, our richness grows. And the greatest love of all is God's love for us. This truth was so important, God sent Jesus to us to let us know that His love transcends all else, and that we can become closer to Him by loving ourselves and others.

I am reminded of a mother who had just fed her toddler the last bit of food they possessed. Now there was nothing left: the cabinets were bare and the refrigerator was empty. The mother folded her hands over her baby's hands and with great faith prayed, "Lord, there is no more food. It is up to You, in Your mercy and love, to care for us."

Thirty minutes later, her doorbell rang. There stood a sweet, smiling lady she had never seen before who said, "I'm newly attending your church, and they told me you lived out my way. I thought we could have some fellowship."

The mother happily invited the lady in and they began to talk of the love of God. After a while, the lady asked for a glass of water. Since the baby was fussing a bit, the mother replied, "Help yourself, there's cold water in the refrigerator," forgetting that there was nothing else.

Soon thereafter, the lady said she had to go and pick up her children from school. An hour later, the doorbell rang again and there was the sweet lady with her four children, each one holding a bag of groceries.

The young mother hugged her and whispered, "Thank You, Lord." That family had nothing left to eat, but three hours later, they had everything they needed . . . all from a stranger who had miraculously appeared at their door.

I have heard it said, "Our loving deeds are the overflow of our love of God from within." That was certainly the case for the hungry mother and her child.

Choose love, my friends, for after I did so, my life changed dramatically, and I have never looked back. It will be the same for you, for when you walk in love, the Lord walks beside you.

BE SELECTIVE WHEN SEEKING
YOUR SOUL MATE

The LORD God said, "It is not good for the man to be alone.
I will make a helper suitable for him." . . . So the LORD God
caused the man to fall into a deep sleep; and while he was
sleeping, he took one of the man's ribs and closed up the place
with flesh. Then the LORD God made a woman from the rib he
had taken out of the man, and he brought her to the man. The
man said, "This is now bone of my bones and flesh of my flesh."

(Genesis 2:18, 21–23 NIV)

The ancient Greeks believed that when you were born your
soul divided in two, and that as you went through life, you would
always be searching for the other half of your soul. They believed
that when you found each other, your hearts would immediately
recognize each other and feel a sense of completion. They pre-
dicted that when you gazed deep within your soul mate's eyes,
you could see a reflection of yourself, for two individuals would
now be as one.

My grandmother always told me, "When the right one comes
along, you'll know it." Then I would question, "How would I
possibly *know*?" Nevertheless, she confidently replied, "Oh, don't
worry—you'll know."

I have to admit, from the very beginning, I knew Todd was
the one for me. He was genuinely kind, faithful, caring, and
helpful. I also instinctively knew he would be a great dad. In

fact, I must say that after eleven years of marriage, I have never seen him angry, raise his voice, or complain.

Todd has been a true gift from God for me and for our three daughters. I fervently wish the same for everyone who is still searching for his or her soul mate, for a lasting source of happiness is a lifelong marriage to the right person.

The Bible says, "A cord of three strands is not quickly broken" (Ecclesiastes 4:12 NIV). In order for a marriage to succeed, there are three threads vital to keeping it together: romance, respect, and reliability. These three ingredients can bind together a husband and a wife in a love that will last a lifetime.

After seventy years of marriage, an elderly Connecticut couple wrote to me about the meaning of reliability and commitment. Together, they share a gold mine of loving memories. As the wife wrote, "After seventy years you go through so much with your partner. Since each one of us has our own personality and habits, it takes love and great patience living with one another. We have been through everything together, from depression to sickness, to birth and death. We have overcome all of these with our abiding love."

Just as a symphony is composed of much more than one note, expect ups and downs in your relationship. Trials and tests will come, but hold on to the treasure of true love. Things have a way of working themselves out for the good, and your relationship will become stronger, richer, and deeper after overcoming hardship. The warmth of your love will comfort you like the rays of the sun after a cold rain.

If you are entering the realm of marriage, do so prayerfully. Search within your heart and be absolutely sure you are with the right one. Don't rush into anything or follow the crowd and act on impulse. Be the wise individual you are and stand strong against temptations to act irrationally. God put His voice into each of us: it's called a *conscience*. Listen to it if you are unsure; it's one of God's many gifts to us.

Marry not for money, looks, or fame. All of these could be lost. Marry only for character. Qualities like absolute trustworthiness, kindness, and devotion will outlast any big bank account, fancy car, or good looks.

Todd proposed to me on New Year's Eve in 1996 and presented me with a lovely diamond engagement ring. The stone was a round solitaire that sat on a simple gold band. Todd and I were so happy and immediately began making plans for a summer wedding.

Newly engaged, I was delighted to share the news with my coworkers the following Monday. To my surprise, some of the young women in the office balked when I held out my left hand, showing them my diamond engagement ring. They peered at my ring as if they couldn't see it. And yes, it was a far cry from the three- and four-karat "rocks" that adorned their fingers, but the size of the ring didn't matter to me. It was the love, trust, and respect with which it was given that warmed my heart.

Anyway, I am now going to share with you something no one knows—not even Todd. A few nights after we were engaged, I had a disturbing dream. In my dream, I was engaged to another man and on my finger was a large solitaire diamond. It was huge; it must have been at least six karats! But the man I was to marry was mean, hot-tempered, and uncaring. He was awful, a far cry from Todd, who is just the opposite, as sweet-natured as any man can be.

I woke up that next morning and exhaled a sigh of relief, so thankful that I was engaged to a wonderful man I knew would be a great husband and, one day, an excellent father. I believe God gave me a glimpse in that dream of what could have been. I give thanks every day that I knew in my heart Todd was the husband God had chosen for me.

When Todd and I got married, we had printed on our ivory wedding invitations: "Love is life's greatest gift, an eternal miracle of God." I wrote these words because God's grace was touching two separate lives and making them one.

All of us want to find our true mates. When you put God first in your life and look for a mate who will do the same, you will find a love everlasting.

WE SHOULD NEVER TAKE LOVE FOR GRANTED

One day, a wife asked her husband as he was reading the newspaper, "Do you love me?"

She heard a few muffled sounds behind the sports section.

"Well," she said, "do you?"

"Mumble, mumble," came from behind the newspaper.

Again, the wife said, "Please tell me that you love me."

Finally, her husband put the paper down and said, "Look, when we got married fifteen years ago, I told you that I loved you. If it ever changes, I'll let you know."

We may laugh when we hear that scenario, but it isn't too far from the truth. All people need to know that they are loved and appreciated, that they are as delightful now as they were long ago.

When was the last time you told your spouse, child, or friend that you loved him or her? If you answered, "Today!" I say, good for you! Now, tell him or her again before the day is through!

Amid all the outside hustle and bustle, there are vulnerable people who need to know that they are admired, respected, and loved. Show those special ones in your life that you are grateful for their company as you continue on your life journey.

This is especially true of your children. You are there to set an example they can follow, so take the time to get down on the floor with them and enter their world of imaginary cars traveling down the highway, or dolls getting ready to go to the dance. Snuggle together on the sofa and read them a story, a poem, or the Sunday comics. They know that when you give your time and attention you are sharing your love with them.

My heart is full as I reminisce about when I was a little girl and my mother and I would walk hand in hand to school every morning. On the weekends, we'd put together puzzles, play cards or hopscotch, and go grocery shopping together, each of us with her own cart. These recollections give me wonderful, lasting memories of days that will never come again.

Usually our very closest friends know we love them because we share everything with them. We laugh together, cry together, and are sympathetic and loyal to one another. Remember, your spouse should be your best friend also. Speak kindly to each other, act with tenderness, hold hands often, correct with gentleness, learn from each other, appreciate the little things, be good to your loved one, and cherish every moment you have together.

Try this idea: tape an encouraging note to the steering wheel of your mate's car. Maybe you can call unexpectedly and extend a surprise invitation to your mate for a romantic picnic lunch at the park. Or bring a single red rose home to say, "I'm thinking of you, my love."

Give a few extra hugs and words of appreciation. When your husband mows the lawn, for example, do you just take it for granted and think, *It's about time?* The next chance you get, give your man a pat on the back and say, "Gee, honey, that lawn looks great!" This combined with an "I love you" will make him feel like a king.

When someone cooks dinner, do you just eat it in silence and then get up from the table and watch television without saying, "Thanks, that was great"? The more you express aloud your appreciation and love, the more love and appreciation you will feel.

And don't forget to thank God. He wants your love, too. Tell Him how much you appreciate all the beauty around you and all the wonderful things that He has blessed you with: home, family, friends, and pets. And as you walk at the seashore or the park and look at the magnificent, multicolored sunset . . . can't you hear Him? He is saying, "Tell Me that you love Me."

OTHERS COME TO KNOW GOD'S LOVE BY YOUR GOOD DEEDS

In this stitch in time, I am writing to you, dear readers, to give my honest testimony of what I have learned about God.

I regularly tell my children that life is like a circle: what goes around comes around. And then I explain, "When you do a good deed, it comes back to you." We read in Ephesians 6:8, "Knowing that whatsoever good thing any man doeth, the same thing shall he receive of the Lord" (Ephesians 6:8 KJV). Love, compassion, and sharing complete the circle as we become the hands of God.

Caring and generosity do not go unnoticed: "The eyes of the LORD run to and fro throughout the whole earth, to show Himself strong on behalf of those whose heart is loyal to Him" (2 Chronicles 16:9 NKJV).

A lady wrote and told me, "Yesterday, I was at the store and a young man with a disability was bagging my groceries and asked me about my own disability. He then said he would keep me in his prayers! I'm still touched to my very soul. Surely, he is an angel unaware." This lady for years has sent little cards with inspiring messages on them to bless others. It isn't how much you do; it is just that you care. You, too, can say a prayer for another. Sometimes, all a person needs is a prayer spoken to begin a phenomenal change of events.

A saying I read attributed to Charles A. Hall reads, "We sow our thoughts and reap our actions. We sow our actions and we reap our habits. We sow our habits and reap our character. We sow our character and we reap our destiny." Thus, let us always treat our friends with love, strangers with kindness, and those who oppose us with patience and understanding—even if it's very hard to do. The doing of good deeds, which is magnified by God Himself, surpasses every other personal enjoyment.

This weekend the weather was very warm, and the girls decided they wanted to sell pink lemonade. They set up a stand in front of our house and made a sign: "Ice-Cold Lemonade: 99 cents a cup!"

Before long, neighbors of ours came by, saying, "How wonderful! We'll have one cup of lemonade, please."

Lauren ecstatically poured the lemonade and handed the cup to the wife.

"Thank you," she said, taking a sip. Then her husband reached in his pocket and gave the girls a twenty-dollar bill. "Put this money in your piggy bank," he said.

Lauren and Gabriella looked at each other and quickly responded, "We are giving the money to charity to help feed children in need."

Afterward, Lauren wrote a letter:

Dear helpers from Feed the Children,

My name is Lauren and I'm soon 10-years-old. I think what you do is really helpful to children in need. One day, I might want to help you with Feed the Children. Right now, I am making a list of different ways to help the poor, like donating food or money or selling things like lemonade and give the money we make to charities like yours.

Love,

Lauren Grace Vigorito

Ponder this: even as children, how people choose to live their lives can be the best witness to God's love.

I am reminded of the sweet story a friend told me about her young son: "Once, I got a call from one of my neighbors. She had been collecting for some charity and had come to the house when I was not yet home from work. My son, who is a very loving and giving person, knew where I kept the household money. He got it and gave it all to her (my money for the whole month!). She was certain that I did not mean for him to give it all to her—so she called me to ask what I would donate and she returned the rest! I was thankful, since we live hand to mouth! But this remains a delightful memory."

There is a charming bed-and-breakfast in our hometown. And instead of a "No Vacancy" sign, when they are at full capacity they have a signpost that reads "Happily Filled." That is how we will feel when we love and help others . . . *happily filled!*

Do you know that when you share a simple smile, it softens stress for others?

What else can you do to show love? Lend an understanding ear. Speak kindly, sincerely, with inspiration to others. Make everything that comes out of your mouth an edifying word of compassion and understanding. The words "I understand; I have been through that," or "I'm going to be with you every step of the way" will be like a balm to the recipient's ears.

Just dial a number and talk to an acquaintance living alone. It doesn't matter what you say, just chatter away, and it will be music to his or her ears. Scripture says, "Rejoice with those who rejoice, and weep with those who weep" (Romans 12:15 NKJV).

Genuine joy and security come from helping those around you in a meaningful way. I believe a happy life is the reward we receive for contributing to others and being a blessing in their lives.

A reader shared with me some very special advice: "Live in such a way that those who know you, but don't know God, will come to know God because of you." What a wonderful world it would be if everyone could practice this.

"God sees your good deeds," I once told my Gabriella. With her two missing front teeth and her eyes bright with love, Gabriella replied, "God sees it, Mommy, and He knows it . . . because *He did it.*"

As the years pass, I think more and more about what truly matters in life. And so many things that once seemed important no longer matter. Helping others and dreaming our dreams full of joyful expectation make life such an adventure.

I heard someone say it like this: acts of love and kindness, when passed from heart to heart, are touches of God's own love from one person to another. Blessed are those who can give without remembering and take without forgetting.

THE FAMILY THAT PRAYS TOGETHER
STAYS TOGETHER

As a newlywed, I did not quite understand . . . but now I do.

A dear friend of mine gave me this wise advice just before I married: "Catherine, do not try to get from each other what you can only get from God."

Did I comprehend the magnitude of her sincere words then? Did I realize the challenges that marriage was going to bring Todd and me? The edges of life can sometimes be rough and jagged, even for the most contented and joy-filled couples. The pressures of extended families, business, daily chores, and inter-actions with others can be overwhelming and sometimes down-right stressful. This is the stuff of life!

Our spouses may be the most wonderful people in the world, but no *one* person can be everything. My mate is only human, and we both must give every need to God, the One who fills the voids. God alone is enough.

His love reveals to you how very important you are and how much you are loved. When you have a deep, abiding, personal knowledge of God's love, your longing for acceptance and un-derstanding will be satisfied.

As a young girl, I would often ask my mother how to have a good marriage. She gave me this simple answer: "Put God first, your spouse second, and yourself third." Marriage is not just a relationship between two people; God must be part of the equation for it to truly succeed.

The changing seasons of romance, combined with the emotions triggered by career and finances, can put stress on any family. Temptations are all around you. Therefore, look to build character by reading God's Word and applying it to your daily lives. Scripture says, "Be imitators of God . . . and walk in love" (Ephesians 5:1–2 NKJV). Taking this walk in love will unite a family for eternity.

Long-married couples have told me that the most important attributes of a successful marriage are respect for God and each other, and a total commitment to building character. We can bring out the best in each other by sharing similar interests but also by giving the other time to pursue individual hobbies. "Never let little annoyances bother you," suggests a woman I know who has been married for fifty years. "The positives can far outweigh any negative force."

A gentleman who just celebrated his fortieth wedding anniversary declared, "I never leave for work without kissing my wife good-bye." And a couple from church who have been married for fifty-five years told me, "Don't let the sun set on an argument. If you have a difference in opinion, patch it up that night."

In God's perfect time, as you both pray to Him, He will smooth the hills and fill the valleys with joy.

Love is always willing to make sacrifices. Todd goes out of his way to help me in every aspect of our life together, whether it's raising the children, doing the housework, or building my career. He always encourages me and helps me pursue my dreams. Even when I have high and lofty goals, he smiles, listens with an understanding heart, and then joins me as we get to work to make them come true!

Speak the sweet language of love to your partner and set a good example for the children's sake, too. Because your children will mirror your actions, the best thing you can give them is the gift of showing love for your partner. In time, they will pass this loving example on to their own spouses and children.

I love what our neighbors just shared with us. Nestled in a little nook on their roof, they showed Todd, the girls, and me a newly constructed bird's nest. We tiptoed under it and saw baby sparrows peeking out from the brush.

"How sweet," I told my neighbors. "The love inside your home reaches beyond its doors." Peace does start in your own home, and as you love one another, that love will stretch in the direction of whoever may need you—even tiny birds.

And at the end of the day, strengthen your marriage by praying together. Every evening, my family and I pray over our meal. After we say our prayers, we all take turns going around the table naming things for which we are thankful. My precious nine-year-old says, "I'm thankful for my sisters," as her little sisters clap and smile gleefully. "I am thankful for our home," says Gabriella. "I'm thankful for Mommy," says Sophia. And Mommy is so thankful for Daddy.

"Let's go around the table again," they all say collectively. Children are tender and sweet, so fresh from heaven. They come absorbed in God's ways and offer His joy so easily. A child's love is pure, genuine, and open to the awesome love of the Father. So let us prepare a place for Him in a home blessed with contentment.

These years we have together are our treasures. A passage in the Bible reads, "What therefore God hath joined together, let not man put asunder" (Matthew 19:6 KJV). I strive to give all my cares to Him, for I am confident, knowing He has our little family encircled in His arms, and the whole world is in His Hands.

OUR DEEPEST LOVE LASTS A LIFETIME

A humble, kind young man fell hopelessly in love at first sight with a lovely young woman. Though they were friends, she hardly took notice of his love for her because the man's face was horribly scarred. Months and then more months passed. The man sent declarations of his love to her, but each time his words were gently declined.

One sunny fall day, as the leaves on the trees were just beginning to change into glorious colors, they walked together in the park. The man asked the young woman, "Do you believe that marriages are made in heaven?"

She was caught off guard, and after a few moments she answered, "Why yes. Do you?"

The man replied, "Most certainly. In heaven, you see, at the birth of each boy, God chooses which girl he should marry and also what afflictions we must overcome to bring forth the beautiful character He has put within us."

Looking deeply into the face of his beloved, the man continued, "When I was born, God pointed out my future bride." With tears in his eyes he said, "But her appearance was to be marred at birth. 'God,' I pleaded, 'let her be beautiful, I beg you. Give me the scars instead.' "

There was a stunned silence as she, for the first time, looked past his scarred face and into the kindest, gentlest, and most loving eyes she had ever seen. The glory of revelation filled the young woman's soul as she had flashing glimpses of the marriage to be, which was once designed in heaven.

True love comes from the heart. Look past every outward appearance and find the treasure of pure character hidden deep within. There can be much more to a person than meets the eye. You'll find it when you seek the depths of another's soul by sharing your own.

Surface beauty lasts and is admired for such a short time. Inner beauty brings devotion, respect, a bond of friendship, and a growing love that will carry two people up to and through eternity.

About eighteen years ago, I dated someone for a short time whom I met through a mutual friend. He was an attorney, came from a wealthy family, and lived in an upscale neighborhood with many advantages. As you know, at the time I lived in a tiny two-room apartment, I had no family money or position, and though he liked me, he was unable to look beyond my present condition. I'm thankful the relationship soon ended.

I always said I would rather live in a cave with someone I loved and who loved me than in a castle with someone I didn't. Though many people suggest to others, "Marry for money," I say, "Marry for love—or stay single."

While it can bring wondrous blessings, marriage isn't for everyone. In the Bible, King David said something similar: "It is better to dwell in a corner of the housetop, than with a brawling woman in a wide house" (Proverbs 21:9 KJV).

Elizabeth Barrett put her feelings so beautifully into a poem that she wrote when she was being courted by her future husband, Robert Browning: "How do I love thee, let me count the ways. I love thee to the depth and breadth and height my soul can reach." And in the last sentence she wrote, "And, if God choose, I shall but love thee better after death."

God planted seeds of love in our hearts. But the key is that they must be constantly watered and fed in order for them to grow. Last week, I forgot to water the plant in our living room, and in just two days it dried up. But when I poured life-giving water on it, almost immediately it sprang up, healthy and alive.

This principle works the same with love and admiration: as you nourish your loved ones by being extravagant with affection and praise, your relationships will bloom and thrive. As Elizabeth Barrett Browning said, love so strong will last into eternity.

PRECIOUS STRANGERS REFLECT GOD'S LOVE

A dear woman, perhaps in her late eighties, approached me while I was sitting quietly in a bookstore. Though I had never seen this woman before, our souls were connected, our hearts linked. And I saw the beauty of the Lord within her, for her blue eyes shone with His love.

In that instant, she took my face gently in her hands and said softly, "I love you . . . with Jesus' love," and then she slowly walked away. With that simple gesture, that woman taught me the power of a stranger's love.

Our eyes always tell the story. The Bible confirms this truth in Matthew 6. It says, "The lamp of the body is the eye. If therefore your eye is good, your whole body will be full of light" (Matthew 6:22 NKJV). Therefore, let your eyes be focused only on doing God's will.

Some time ago, I read about Mother Teresa's Home for the Dying, which cared for people who were very ill and had nowhere to turn. The home was in Calcutta, and Mother Teresa and her sisters would bring in the poorest and most desperately ill people from the street. Taking their sick bodies inside, they took care of them until the men and women passed away. Mother Teresa said, "They must feel wanted, loved. They are Jesus for me."

Early one April evening, we were at a local eatery celebrating Todd's birthday. We were just finishing our dinner and the girls were coloring pictures in coloring books at our table. Out of the blue, a golden-haired girl, wearing a pink frilly dress, walked up to us and with a smile, joined in and started coloring with my children, as if she had known us for years.

She was warm and friendly, and I asked her between sips of coffee, "What's your name?"

With a grin she replied, lifting her head from coloring her picture, "It's Paige."

Her parents gave a nod of approval from a few tables over as Paige began to chat and giggle with our Sophia.

Paige stayed with us for the remainder of the evening, and when it was time to leave, she hugged each one of us good-bye. "God bless you," I said, waving.

"We don't see that every day," Gabriella acknowledged as walked out the front door of the restaurant. I squeezed her ha. and answered, "You know what, Gabriella, we *should* see tha each day!"

Not far from our home there is a flower stand, and for three dollars you can purchase a bouquet of exquisitely colorful flowers. I stopped one day to buy flowers for a neighbor, and to my surprise, there was no one attending the stand, just the beautiful bouquets and a jar for the money. I was moved to leave a nice donation, for whoever left those flowers trusted that people would be at their best in the presence of beauty.

There is a delightful quote from painter Vincent van Gogh that I like so much I am passing it on to you: "Love many things, for therein lies the true strength, and whosoever loves much performs much, and can accomplish much, and what is done in love is done well."

A mother recently wrote that when her young son could never pass anyone collecting money without urging her to give. He knew where the collectors were located in all the stores and ran to them when they shopped. He was so happy to give!

As you minister through living your life under God's grace, sharing His love with others, don't be surprised when precious strangers come up to you and say, "I love you . . . with Jesus' love."

TRUE FRIENDS LEAVE FOOTPRINTS
ON YOUR HEART

Sometimes God gives us one precious person with whom we can share our feelings: one person we can lean on in times of despair and talk to when we need gentle reassurance. And we know that together we are of one heart, one mind, and one accord.

Do you have such a friend?

This person may be a trusted companion, a wise teacher, a sincere relative, a mentor, a soul mate, or a true supporter whose spirit of gentleness, genuine empathy, and tender advice comfort when you need it most. You know the kind of person I'm describing—one who has extraordinary faith, who is remarkable in the giving of self and time, and who shares wisdom and love unconditionally at any hour.

Offering trust, support, and unconditional love, real friends are your sounding board, your safe haven, and a reflection of who you are, where you have been, and where you are going. I am blessed to have such a person in my life.

"Always follow your own instincts," she would advise when I had a tough decision to make.

"Say a prayer and put your faith in God," she'd say when I felt anxious.

"Take it one step at a time," her soothing voice on the phone would suggest when my patience was ebbing away and despair stood at the ready.

"Catherine, please do not be concerned. God is with you. He has never let you down," she lovingly encouraged when I was overwhelmed with mounting difficulties.

And "I love you and so does God."

How true it is: "A good friend multiplies your strengths and divides your sorrow."

Everyone who accomplishes something extraordinary has had encouragement from someone. In the Bible we are told that Jesus had a close support group, and one disciple, John, offered Him an exceptional friendship: It was he "whom Jesus loved" (John 13:23 NKJV) and with whom the crucified Jesus entrusted the care of His mother.

We all need that special person we can count on, no matter what. Bonds of love and friendship are of utmost value in creating a deeper meaning in our own lives.

There is a saying: "The miracle of love is that love is given to us to give to one another." So if you don't have someone whom you can love and rely upon, ask God to bring someone to you. And even those who are in lonely places can have the most glorious friendship of all, their friendship with God. His is the one love you cannot do without. If you feel abandoned or alone, remember, "There is a friend who sticks closer than a brother" (Proverbs 18:24 NKJV). Nothing can separate you from the love of God. You are His creation, His magnificent work of art.

I reflect on a precious friend, Ruth, who has a special way of expressing God with her wisdom, faithfulness, and loyalty. I think of another dear one, Gia, who has the gift of helpfulness and compassion; and Kim, a vivacious person who has the gift of joyful hope and faith. I chuckle when I think of the warm and welcoming smile that always adorns her lovely face.

Although we have never met, a long-distance friend is like a sister to me with her warmth, support, and advice. In addition, I think of another friend who is blessed with extraordinary talents, thoughtfulness, and genuine caring. We are of one heart, one mind, and one accord.

Being a friend to someone is one of the best gifts you could give, reaching out in love and in kindness. The key? Show your friends how much you care, and you will have friends for life!

Try this: at the beginning of the day, affirm, *Today, I will make at least one person's life a little better, happier, or brighter.* Then, follow through on all your generous desires to help or inspire another. When you open your heart to assist someone you embody the grace of God, and deeds of kindness will flow from you. Soon, this manner of giving will become second nature to you. By being a living expression of God's kindness, courteous to all, you become His hands, His eyes, and His feet. Last week, a friend of mine read a bumper sticker that said, "One man can make a difference. . . . Jesus did." What a wonderful example for us all!

If you want to know the type of person you are, evaluate your friends. Do they drag you down because you no longer think alike? If so, it is time to find other friends who will encourage you to reach greater heights.

I think of King David, who God said was "a man after His own heart" (1 Samuel 13:14 NKJV). David's thoughts and motivations must have matched God's desires. That's why it's good to talk to an all-powerful and wise heavenly Father—a Friend who will kiss your forehead and take your worries away. He always gives peace in the midst of the storm.

God also wants you to have close friends as you travel life's highway. Eleanor Roosevelt wrote, "Many people will walk in and out of your life, but only true friends will leave footprints on your heart."

At this very moment, express gratitude to God for someone

who has enriched your life in an extra-special way. Then, tell that person how much you love and appreciate him or her. By doing so, you will have begun a chain of goodness that can be passed on and on and on.

Let us be . . . "like-minded, having the same love, being of one accord, of one mind" (Philippians 2:2 NKJV).

"JUST BE HAPPY," AS YOUR LOVED ONES WANT YOU TO BE

Sophia smiled broadly, her hair in two cute ponytails. She came running into my open arms, laughing and saying, "Mommy, I'm so, so happy."

I laughed with pure joy as I hugged her close and said, "Nothing could make me happier than your being happy, my special child."

Suddenly I recalled my own dear mother's words to me, "My darling child, I just want you to be happy."

Perhaps I never really understood a mother's love until now—how rare, how sacred. I think mothers were brought about by God to show us that He loves us unconditionally and eternally. Motherhood is a sacred duty. It requires strength of character so we can form our children's character.

Certainly I could never explain the loss I felt when I sat in my room on the day of my mother's funeral. Three days before, she was alive and vibrant, making plans for the weekend, and then suddenly she was gone forever.

And I found myself expecting that at any moment she would walk into the room, smiling, vivacious, and comforting. And sometimes, even now, though twenty-one years have passed, I still think she will.

I was quite taken with a letter I received from a seventeen-year-old student who recently lost her beloved mother. Her words echoed in my heart as I read, "My mother and I were best friends, and she taught me lessons I will carry with me forever. Although I still can't accept her death, I am now ready to face any obstacles that come my way because I know she would want that."

On Mother's Day this year, I phoned this young woman. "Thank you for writing to me and for sharing your beautiful letter," I said, "and I am so sorry about your mom. . . . I know how you feel."

I went on to tell her that I felt those who are gone are not lost but live with us forever. The memories of their words, the warmth of their smiles, and the love they gave us are alive in our hearts, providing comfort. My tears fell onto her letter as I affirmed, "Your mom is just a thought away, and her wisdom can continue to give you strength for the rest of your life."

She could barely speak, whispering, "I am so sad, but in this life, I feel God doesn't give you anything you cannot handle."

I agreed and said, "You know, I've heard it said that death is far from being the end. It is an open door to an existence larger, brighter, and more blessed than this. Upon leaving this earth, there is a world of endless sunshine, for we are children of God's Light. His ultimate design for us is to have His love and live with Him eternally."

She paused for a moment, then agreed, "Yes, you're right. And thank you, Catherine."

We both sat with our thoughts for a moment. Before we said our good-byes, I said, "Your mother would want you to be happy." Then we hung up, both of us feeling the connection be-tween ourselves, our absent mothers, and God's love.

Whenever I hear my mother's voice saying, "Catherine, I just want you to be happy," the memory of her life moves me forward. My mother's face was the first one that I recognized, her calming voice was the one that told me bedtime stories, and her arms were the ones that rocked me to sleep. Though years have passed, I still see her and feel her love—a love I will never forget.

I know that she still watches over us all as I gaze upward and say to her in a whisper, a prayer, and in praise, "Yes, Mom, I am happy. Thank you for my life."

THE GREAT ONES ARE THOSE WHO REMAIN HUMBLE

The Bible says, "He who is greatest among you shall be your servant" (Matthew 23:11 NKJV).

God gives such grace to the meek and humble individual whose greatest desire is to be of help to others. The person who is the most attentive to others is usually the most blessed.

Many years ago, I had an appointment to meet and interview a world-famous author for an upcoming column and television segment. Driving to his Connecticut residence, I wondered what kind of home this famous man would live in. I imagined a huge mansion, a six-car garage, and massive gates.

As I drove up his long driveway, I saw his house. To my sur-prise, it was sweet and humble, nestled in the woods, surrounded by God's free-flowing nature, with birds cheerily singing and squirrels scampering. I was suddenly eager to meet this man.

He answered the door dressed in a comfortable, casual outfit, a warm smile on his face and arms outstretched. I will never forget those wonderful, joy-filled hours. Of all his good qualities, his desire to serve others made the biggest impression on me.

With my mini tape recorder in hand, we strolled around his house while I asked him scores of questions. His answers conveyed his philosophies: "Life is a constant opportunity to assist others." "The more you help someone, the further you can go."

Suddenly he said, "Catherine, you have been through a lot in your life."

I think a look of surprise came across my face as I asked, "How can you judge that by one meeting?" I had never seen this man before.

Our eyes met and he said, "Why else would you want to help people as you do?" He then explained that problems alter your life and love emerges from it. "Excuse me a minute," he said and disappeared into an adjoining room. He returned with something in his hand. "This is for you," he offered, extending it to me.

It was a pin that read: "You make a difference."

Touched, I said softly, "I appreciate *you*."

Toward the end of our visit, I thanked Dr. Bernie Siegel for his time and kindness and left.

As I backed out of the driveway, I stopped my car for a moment to look back at him in the doorway. His wife had joined him, along with their dog, and we waved good-bye. And I pondered, *Alone we can do little, but together we can do so much.*

Todd was away for a few days on a business trip. While I was in the kitchen putting away some groceries, Lauren said to me, "Mommy, with Daddy away, can I be in charge?"

I said, "Sure, honey, but I do expect you to help me with your little sisters . . . like you always do." Lauren's eyes danced and she asked, "Can I tell them what to do?" To my amazement, I knew I was being gifted with a perfect time to explore an important life lesson with her. "Lauren, honey," I said, "leaders are chosen to serve."

Then, suddenly inspired, I got down on my knees, looked up at her, and replied, "Leaders look up to people, as I am doing from this position, and they put others first and help them along."

After that, I stood up and looked over her head, saying, "True leaders never look down on others or meanly demand, belittle, or abuse others with their authority." Lauren listened intently, and I believe this simple analogy made my daughter understand.

Then I told her that the Bible says, "Blessed are the merciful, for they will be shown mercy" (Matthew 5:7 NIV); and "Whatever you do or say, do it as a representative of the Lord" (Colossians 3:17 NLT).

Quietly Lauren went upstairs to the playroom, picked out a game that her sisters would both enjoy, and sat down on the floor to play with them.

The secure, confident person never feels the need to impress people with his or her ability, worldly goods, rank, or status. When we seek only our own way, we make the mistake of thinking we're superior. A negative attitude toward our fellow human beings will never bring success.

The key is to always try to get along with people. I read somewhere that a study showed business success largely lies in one's ability to get along with people. A personal manager of a large organization said that one of the main reasons employees are discharged or leave companies is because they cannot get along with others.

In Matthew 22, a lawyer asks Jesus, "Teacher, which is the greatest commandment in the law?" (Matthew 22:36 NKJV). Jesus replied, " 'You shall love the LORD your God with all your heart, with all your soul, and with all your mind.' . . . And the second is like it: 'You shall love your neighbor as yourself' " (Matthew 22:37–39 NKJV). Jesus said that on these two commandments hung all the Law and the Prophets. This means that love has unequaled power, filling the whole law of successful living.

Sometimes people are trapped in a shell that was formed by their childhood. Many of these people are what I call "turtles," hard on the outside but soft on the inside. Don't judge the shell, because maybe within that shell is an exquisite person.

God can always make us into new creations: His lovely sons and daughters, meant to dwell in the highest of heavens, where happiness is His throne.

Last year, I was at my local fitness center when out of the corner of my eye I saw a man lifting weights. His arms were covered in tattoos. I noticed this but did not think much about it; but the next day, to my surprise, he approached me.

"Catherine?" he said.

"Yes," I answered, wondering what this tattooed man and I might have in common.

"I just wanted to say that my wife and I enjoy your writing very much. Your words have helped us both tremendously."

"Thank you! That is nice of you to say," I replied, shaking his hand, again marveling at how many forms God's lessons may take.

Since that time, wherever I see that man, we talk a bit about life and the challenges we all encounter. He is very wise, full of faith, and a very kind person. The experience also taught me never to judge people by their appearances.

A while back, a reader shared a Native American prayer that says, "Grant that I may not criticize my neighbor until I have walked a mile in his moccasins." Evangelist Dwight L. Moody said, "Be humble or you'll stumble."

What made Princess Diana so revered? It was not the fact that she was famous or beautiful, but the fact that she, even as royalty, humbled herself. In love she hugged the leper, held the dying, and comforted the maimed and ill. Those were the acts that made her a woman to respect and honor.

Take the biblical advice that says, "He who humbles himself will be exalted" (Matthew 23:12 NKJV). God is in a position to exalt you to the greatest heights and give you your heart's desire. When you live in His name, you can trust that He will respond with all His love.

FIND THE PLACE WHERE YOUR GREATEST LOVE MEETS THE WORLD'S GREATEST NEED

Every day, extraordinary deeds are performed by ordinary people like you and me to make the world a better place. One person, with one idea, with a single act of genuine kindness, can make a difference.

I once heard an interesting quote from a minister as he spoke of the best way to true happiness: "Find the place where your greatest love meets the world's greatest need."

What is it that you love most?

Today, Lauren is learning to play the flute in the school band.

One afternoon, as she was finished practicing for the school's upcoming concert, she asked, "Do you think I would be good at the clarinet next year?"

Without hesitation I replied, "I think you would be good at anything you put your heart and mind to." Sure enough, Lauren began learning how to play the clarinet, and she loved every minute of it! Love what you do and pass that love on to others—that is the key!

Do you know that you have the ability to achieve the impossible if you believe and put your whole heart into what you'd like to accomplish for the good of humankind? God will bless you abundantly as you determine to forge ahead to help others and make the world a better place in which to live.

Scripture says, "Whatever you do, work at it with all your heart, as working for the Lord, not for men" (Colossians 3:23 NIV).

Great painters express love for God's beautiful earth. Auguste Renoir was almost paralyzed by arthritis, but when asked why he continued to paint when he was in such agony, he gently replied, "The beauty remains; the pain passes."

Those who are memorable have expressed their love for all humankind. Abraham Lincoln, born in poverty in a one-room log cabin, refused to let an undistinguished background stop him. He prevailed over personal struggles, financial difficulties, defeats, and depression. Honest and hardworking, Lincoln overcame numerous obstacles and became one of the greatest presidents in history, an instrument to free the lives of millions.

Great inventors express the love of creativity, curiosity, and vision. The Wright brothers went through tremendous trouble on their way to success. It took Wilber and Orville Wright years of intense studying and countless experimenting, cycles of emotional ups and downs, and refusing to listen to doubters, before they achieved success on December 17, 1903, at Kitty Hawk, North Carolina, with the Wright Flyer.

Victory is ahead for those who have inspiration and proceed with love and determination, continuing to work hard; and for those who have suffered defeat, yet never let it stop them.

I know a woman who was born into poverty and then was orphaned as a child, along with her sister. With limited resources but unlimited love in her heart, she decided not to settle for the norm. She wanted to do more with her life, more for her sister, more for humanity.

So with the faith in God she had learned as a child, she met her trials with trust and prayer. Each morning she prayed for guidance and for God's perfect will. She believed that when people pray, things happen. As a result, she prayed with expectation, seeking to serve, and had faith that she would find her way around her challenges and obstacles.

This young woman worked hard, earned good grades, and with the help of an encouraging mentor, secured a scholarship and went on to college.

She loved children and teaching, and today she is a foster mother and a remarkable teacher, inspiring countless students. She explained to me once, "As a result of all my trials, my faith was strengthened and my love and compassion were increased."

Whatever we pursue, we must do it with all our hearts. We never ask for the challenges that life places at our feet, but as we continue to move forward, we discover these very obstacles are forming our strength, character, and courage.

One summer, while the family and I were vacationing in Cape Cod, I read an article about Albert Schweitzer. It said that at the age of thirty, Schweitzer went back to school as a student of medicine. This doctor of philosophy, doctor of theology, accomplished organist, and famous writer knew he must have a medical degree to help cure illnesses and more knowledgeably help the people in Africa achieve better health. The years were strenuous for him, but after six years of medicine, he passed his final test. From that time on, Schweitzer lovingly devoted himself to helping suffering humankind.

Despite the obstacles, mistakes, or setbacks that you face, continue to love and believe in yourself. Keep persevering and trying your best, bringing forth the exceptional talents that God has given you to bless the lives of others. As you follow your heart, stretch your faith and broaden your vision. Then, as you extend a helping hand to others, you will discover newfound strength and abilities within yourself.

If you have a loving and willing heart, God will help you "find the place where your greatest love meets the world's greatest need."

He can and He will.

RAISE CHILDREN LOVINGLY IN TODAY'S WORLD

As I sit by the picture window, my mind drifts back, recalling the moments I first held my sweet babies in my arms. They have been our greatest blessing and our constant delight.

Divine miracles, fresh from heaven, they marvel us with all their charming ways. How can I forget their extraordinary smiles, first words, and enchanting mannerisms? They are the wonder of our lives.

This year, our oldest sweet girl will turn ten. I feel joy mingled with a trace of melancholy as I consider this amazing child. She has an incredible ability to adapt to new situations and surroundings. As I watch her develop into the person she will be, I pray that the good Lord will gently lead her onto the right paths as she goes into the world where other lives and contrary forces will influence her life.

While watching a popular children's movie when she was three years old, she said during a scary scene, "Mommy, let's throw this video out. Let's mail it away." I realized that in our modern world, we can be unaware what is creeping into children's minds and hearts. We think that if everybody else watches it, it's all right. It isn't.

Parenthood is a vocation, a calling, a revered trust. Caring for children requires patience, unconditional love, and steadfast perseverance. Scripture states, "Train up a child in the way he should go, and when he is old he will not depart from it" (Proverbs 22:6 NKJV).

What we are and what we do will create the entire social population of tomorrow. So let us give our children the very best of what we know of God's love, and they will create a better world for the future.

Love to children is spelled in the days, hours, and minutes we spend with them. A client of mine once told me how, as a teenager, his son got into trouble with drugs. "I worked all the time," he revealed regretfully. "I was never there for him."

Careers are important, but your children are your precious trust. They need you. Try to help out at their schools, go on their field trips, attend their games, concerts, and dance classes. Slow down and talk and walk with them instead of running away from them.

A mother of two reminded me, "Children do not have to be occupied every minute. They need quiet time, because that is when they can *dream*." We need not overwhelm our children with materialistic comforts to make them happy. A safe, secure environment, along with our time, attention, and genuine love for life, can give our precious children treasures that will outlast the latest game or video craze.

Turn off the television and go on an adventure. Todd and I like to pack a picnic lunch and take the children to the park, let them feed the ducks, and watch the little squirrels gather their food and store it for the winter. Take your family to the zoo, the museum, or the library.

Sometimes we'll all go on a nature walk where the girls collect things along the way. Afterward they glue the items on colored paper and we have original works of art to tack onto the refrigerator, filling the artists with pride and joy. And there's nothing more satisfying than planting a tree or a garden and watching a seed become a beautiful plant.

Only by our examples of unwavering faithfulness, gentleness, and rational decision making will our children take these models of behavior and make them their own.

Sitting under a towering emerald-green oak, I explained to my girls, "The tree began as a tiny acorn and grew patiently and majestically. And you can, too, with patience and wisdom, grow big and strong and become a gift to others."

There are so many joys in raising children: glistening moments, lasting and joyous memories. Our hearts are filled with pride, and my heart overflows with thanksgiving to God for these precious ones.

And as for me, I think over my existence and instruct my

darling daughters to an even higher and better goal, nurturing their awareness of the best life has to offer.

I hope God grants me enough years to meet and enjoy grandchildren, cradle them in my arms, and delight myself in their being a young extension of my own joy-filled life.

For I know that this love is for eternity.

LOVE: Key to Your Heart's Desire

○━━ Love is patient and kind. It keeps the unpleasant things quiet. Whatever problem you may encounter, know that approaching it in the spirit of love will help you solve it. Love conquers all. . . . It always trusts, hopes, and perseveres. Let love be your highest aim.

○━━ You were created to love and to be loved. There is a miraculous power in two, for God's love is at the heart of true friendship. Spending time with real friends can do remarkable things.

○━━ Express love to others through the kindness of your eyes, the sincerity of your words, and the touch of your hand. Love automatically brings blessings and joys that are unmatched.

○━━ God helps each of us when we try to help somebody else. Loving others puts beauty in each of our days, warmth in our homes, and joy in our memories. When we love, we experience the joy of love growing within us.

o—★ The most valuable things are *those people* who are in your life. There are people who love you very much but may not know how to express their feelings. Help them by setting an example. Decide today to be more open in showing your love.

o—★ Become the poster child for unconditional love. Return anger with love and watch anger dissolve. Respond to good things with joy and applaud them. Receive kindness with an appreciative smile. Be a light for others, and watch as your own life is renewed.

o—★ You have only this moment, like a melting snowflake in your hand. Make the most of it by bringing a miracle to someone else. Generosity does not go unnoticed.

Key #7:
FORGIVENESS

If ye forgive men their trespasses,
your heavenly Father will also forgive you.

(Matthew 6:14 KJV)

In the Bible Peter asks, "Lord, how often should I forgive someone who sins against me? Seven times?" Peter thought he was being more than generous until he heard God's answer. "No, not seven times," Jesus replied, "but seventy times seven!" (Matthew 18:21–22 NLT).

Did you know that you can completely destroy the ability of the enemy to hurt you by totally forgiving others? Forgiveness is freedom! It is vital to your own eternal happiness, for without it, your life can be governed by an endless cycle of resentment and retaliation.

The American Heritage Dictionary defines *forgiveness* as: "To excuse a fault or offense, to renounce resentment against." Letting go of a grudge can be one of the best things you can do for yourself.

As you will discover in this chapter, forgiveness is a choice you can freely make—a gift you can give or withhold. Think about it this way: do you want to feel free or remain in the bondage of negative thoughts and feelings?

Forgiving another will bring you the sweetest feeling of pure joy—and relief!—you'll have experienced in a long time. As soon as you release your hostility, bitterness, or anger, it will be replaced by a sense of cleansing and hope—all signs of a glorious new beginning.

There are times when we all need to be forgiven. Remember when you were forgiven of your faults? God has a sea of forgiveness into which He throws all your sins when you confess them, and on the shore of that sea is a sign that reads "No Fishing." Thus, forgive . . . and then forget and move on.

START BY PUTTING ASIDE THE PAIN
FROM YOUR PAST

Throughout life, things come to us that we will never understand. Yes, we make mistakes and bad decisions and get our feelings hurt. But what is most important is how we choose to deal with these wounds.

First we must break free of the pain and the mistakes of the past. Regardless of the challenges now before us, we have been placed here to do great things. God wishes our futures to be filled with immeasurable joy, fulfillment, and victory. But if our hearts are burdened by anger and resentment and we're stuck in the past, we don't have the freedom to move into His future—the future God has waiting for us.

Each morning, I call my dear friend Ray, who is like a father to me. One day while we were talking, he casually asked, "Catherine, have you ever had your house blessed?"

Pausing for a moment, I replied, "No, we haven't. Should we?" I am always open to blessing, for whatever reason, but having my home blessed had never occurred to me! We had moved here four years ago, and though I often said a blessing beneath the cross that hung in our foyer, we had never had a minister formally "bless the house."

"Honey," Ray tenderly said, "I don't want to tell you what to do. But I believe you should have your house blessed. You try so hard, you are such a wonderful person, but I think something is blocking your future success."

I think so much of Ray and highly respect his opinion, so the next day I called our minister and asked if we could make an appointment for him to visit and bless our home.

"Sure, Catherine, I would love to," the minister replied. "Let's set a date and time now." After I set up the time with the minister, I called Ray. "Guess what?" I announced. "The minister is scheduled to be here next Friday!"

Ray was pleased, but then he said something that I will never forget: "Catherine, what I am going to suggest to you now is very important. Before the minister blesses your home, you must *forgive* everyone who has hurt you in the past."

Rather surprised, I thought, *Am I holding grudges? Am I bitter toward those who have intentionally hurt me?*

Appreciating his wise counsel, I agreed, "As always, you are right. I will do exactly as you suggest. I will forgive."

Then Ray shared this philosophy: "Forgiveness can be achieved in one of two ways: by commitment with intent to resume prior relationships, or by commitment with intent to discontinue that association."

I replied, "I am so blessed to have you in my life!" Then I walked outside, slowly strolling down our driveway to the mailbox. With each step, my mind moved backward in time, and I thought of the many people who had hurt me . . . the so-called friends, dishonest people in business, those I had trusted, strangers who had an ax to grind, even relatives. I had been through so much. . . .

Walking back up the driveway, I realized that forgiveness might not be easy. *Can we find the place that God has for us when we can't seem to get over a hurt, or if we are carrying a grievance?* I wondered.

A week later, the minister arrived and the girls happily ran outside to greet him. It was a gorgeous summer afternoon, sunny and warm, so we all sat at our picnic table on the back deck, sipped iced tea, and talked for a while. About thirty minutes later, the house blessing, "Celebration for a Home," began.

The girls, Todd, and I assembled in the living room, and the minister handed each of us a written sheet of paper so we could follow along. The service commenced with a passage from the gospel. After that, I did as Ray suggested, and I silently *forgave* everyone who had hurt me in the past. To my amazement, a wave of pure joy washed over me!

Then we moved from room to room. In the foyer we prayed, "The Lord shall watch over your going out and coming in."

And in the office: "Teach us, O Lord, where wisdom is found, and show us the place of understanding."

In the kitchen: "You shall eat in plenty and be satisfied, and praise the name of the Lord your God, who has dealt wondrously with you."

Next in the bedrooms: "Guide us waking, O Lord, and guard us sleeping, that awake we may watch with Christ, and in sleep we may rest in peace."

After that, holy water was sprinkled in each room.

The ceremony was beautiful. The prayers we said, the forgiveness released, the unfairness forgotten—the peace and joy Todd and I felt were wonderful.

Shortly after, phenomenally, circumstances did begin to change for the better for me, new doors of opportunity started to open . . . and the harmonious, liberating experience of having our home blessed will be one I will forever carry with me.

The key, I believe, is that blessings cannot flow when you

are in a state of anger and resentment. Someone put it like this: "To make forgiveness complete, you must add the word *forget*." And I, for one, found that was true as the warmth of God's love washed away all my hurt.

I have shared my house blessing experience because it worked for me. In whatever way you are able to forgive, whether through a house blessing or by writing a letter that you—and you alone— will read, remember that the twin keys to moving on are the words *forgive* and *forget*.

HAND YOUR HURTS OVER TO GOD

This weekend, the girls, Todd, and I took a walk deep in our backyard and started collecting rocks for a garden project.

The country air was sweet as I bent over and picked up one rock and then another and gently placed them in the wheelbarrow. With the fullness of summer upon us, I felt the sun warm my back as I stooped down to pick up one more.

Then the girls followed suit, and one after another they diligently helped gather the rocks. Within a short time, the wheelbarrow was filled to the top with stones, both big and small.

As Todd carefully wheeled the heavy wheelbarrow back to our house, and I looked at the heaping pile of rocks, I remembered a letter that I received from a dear gentleman who had recently written to me, saying he knew he had been clinging to past hurts.

He went on to tell me in his note of a memorable story that his sister-in-law told him. She had once read about a person who, whenever insulted or treated badly, would bend over and pick up a stone to keep track of the hurt. Over the years, as you can imagine, this person had collected quite a pile of stones!

Reminiscing, this gentleman wrote that he, too, had gathered many stones . . . to his regret. Each stone brought to mind a painful memory, and so he thought of them over and over. The weight of these memories eventually became onerous.

Finally, he said, God enabled him to forgive each hurt. The stones no longer remind him of pain, and his emotional scars are healing. Now when someone throws a stone, he still picks it up—but he gives it to God.

Like my wise correspondent, you, too, can turn to God and say, "Lord, Your Word tells me, 'Give all your worries and cares to God, for he cares about you' (1 Peter 5:7 NLT). So I now leave them in Your divine care."

Place your past disappointments, worries, and cares in God's outstretched arms. Give them over to Him, because He can look ahead to where you cannot, and He loves to show Himself strong in your behalf.

Many years ago, a couple I'm acquainted with unknowingly got involved with someone unscrupulous in business. The person deeply hurt and deceived them. This honest, hardworking team had to endure years of frustration and pain, losing money and valuable time, because of one person's dishonesty and deceitfulness.

After she became physically ill because of the situation, the wife told me how she got down on her knees one evening and prayed, "Lord, I have done all I can. I now release this to You." She implored, "You have seen our hurts and pain and each time we have been mistreated, but I am forgiving that man who has hurt us and trusting You to work this out according to Your way of wisdom."

From then on, she released the bitterness she was holding in her heart and vowed not to strike back in anger at the man who had hurt them. Instead, she filled her mind with positive, productive, and fruitful thoughts and actions.

After three years, this woman told me how God removed that person from their lives and subsequently gave this couple a wonderful new start. In fact, an opportunity came across their paths soon thereafter that quickly propelled them farther ahead than they had ever been on their journey to business success.

When you are walking down the road of life, there will always be challenges that loom ahead, but there will also be that unseen, loving, strong hand to guide you along the way. So when someone throws a stone at you now, bend over, pick it up . . . and hand it to God.

FORGIVENESS IS A CHOICE YOU MAKE

When you encounter people or circumstances that cause you pain, you face two choices: you can either aggravate the situation with a spirit of revenge and bitterness, or you can lubricate your life with the oil of forgiveness and trust in God.

"I forgive you" can be three of the most important words you'll ever say because when you put others' wrongdoings behind you, your own life will be positively transformed.

Let go of bitterness. Release anger. Forget those grievances. Think about it this way: for every one minute you remain resentful or bitter, you lose sixty seconds of tranquility and happiness. Holding a grudge hurts only *you*. Harboring resentment is like hanging on to a virus; you are the only one who feels it, and the other party involved might not even know about it—or even care!

Are you annoyed with someone? Try this: step into that other person's shoes. Realize that we all make mistakes, and focus on the individual's good qualities. Seek to understand, from their point of view, what makes them do the things that make you angry. Then share your feelings with them in a calm, genuine manner. After that, move on, and don't bring up the situation again.

Do you realize that nursing a grievance can actually affect your well-being? Negative emotions can twist your personality into something you don't want or like . . . and injure those around you, too, including the people you never meant to hurt.

I once read a story about a little boy who had a bad temper. One day, the boy's father had an idea: he gave him a hammer and a bag of nails and walked him outside to the white picket fence in front of their farm. "Every time you lose your temper, son," the father instructed, "hammer a nail into this fence."

As the weeks went by, the boy did as the father asked. Soon he began to control his temper, and the number of nails he had to hammer dwindled.

But the lesson was not over. The father took the boy outside one morning and said, "Son, for each day you are able to control your temper, pull one nail out of the fence." A month later, all the nails were removed. But what was remarkable to me was what happened next. . . .

Hand in hand, the father and son walked outside. They looked at the fence, and the father praised the boy for doing so well. "You have learned to control your anger, son, and I am proud of you."

Then the father continued. "However, my son, look at the

holes in the fence." The boy nodded stiffly. "It will never be the same, for when you say things in anger, they will leave a scar, just like these holes from the hammering."

A few months ago, Todd, the girls, and I met good friends of ours and their three children for dessert at an ice-cream shop a few towns over. As the children rode a carousel nearby, my friend and I sat alone at a wooden picnic table and talked.

"It was a turning point in our relationship," revealed Danielle. "My husband and I had been fighting about many things, and our marriage was struggling."

And then the unthinkable happened. "I'll never forget it," she said softly with tear-filled eyes. "I got a phone call at work to say our son had been hit by a car! And in my mind, I thought worst-case scenario: a brain injury."

There was a long pause, then she continued, "Thinking back, my husband and I were even fighting the morning of the accident. But we somehow came together for our son to try to be supportive for him."

Danielle told how her frightened little five-year-old was taken by ambulance to the hospital and admitted to the pediatric intensive care unit. The boy was in excruciating pain. His left leg was broken and required a plate and pins to repair it. The child was in a wheelchair for a month. Then, eight months after the accident the plate and the pins were removed.

"It was definitely a trying and challenging year for our son and our entire family," she told me. "Each morning, I thank God that he's alive and doing well and is a strong, healthy boy."

Danielle looked over at our children, who were merrily riding the carousel, and said, "I never met the man who hit my son, and I do believe it was an accident. Certainly the driver must feel bad, for it has to weigh on his mind."

I grasped her hand as Danielle went on. "God works behind the scenes, and this, I feel, has helped my family grow. Every day is a gift and not to be taken for granted. Forgiving someone is hard to do, but I make mistakes and I need forgiveness from God, so who am I to hold a grudge?"

Forgiveness lends such grace to our character. Scripture says, "Judge not, and ye shall not be judged: condemn not, and ye shall not be condemned: forgive, and ye shall be forgiven" (Luke 6:37 KJV).

Are you asking yourself, *How can I forgive?* Know this: God has seen your struggles. He knows your pain. When you can stand strong in the face of adversity and ask Him for His help, He will open the door to deliver you from hardship and resentment.

In His parable of the unmerciful servant, Jesus tells the story of an honorable king who forgave a servant who owed him ten thousand talents. The servant was not able to pay him back, so the king took pity on him, and with compassion in his heart, the king forgave him the debt.

However, the servant then did not forgive a fellow servant who owed him a small amount of money. Even though the fellow servant begged him, saying, "Have patience with me and I will pay you all" (Matthew 18:26 NKJV), the servant refused and would not forgive.

Some other servants saw what had happened and were saddened. They told the king that the forgiven servant was unmerciful and did not forgive as he had been forgiven.

The king said to the unmerciful servant, "Should you not also have had compassion on your fellow servant, just as I had pity on you?" (Matthew 18:33 NKJV). Then the king sent him to prison until he repaid his entire debt.

This story is actually depicting God as the king who forgives us, His servants. He also expects us to forgive one another as we have been forgiven. So if God says to forgive, then return love for hate, replace bitterness with compassion, and reject resentment in favor of understanding. As you forgive, you will be forgiven.

Recently a gentleman wrote to me explaining that he was unfairly taken out of a long-term, successful career by people who misused their power. With a family to support, he lost his livelihood and began to be consumed by bitter, negative thoughts concerning these people. He lost sleep and grew despondent over his relentless desire for revenge. A bout with depression finally drove him to a doctor's office.

Studies have shown that stress has been linked to a variety of health problems, ranging from headaches to heart attacks. Being full of resentment toward others generates stress, stunts your emotional and spiritual growth, and steals your creativity, your happiness, and your health. But by forgiving, you can turn aside anger's poisonous power.

One day, the man decided not to live in anger anymore. He changed his focus from how he was mistreated to being grateful for the presence of God in his life. Although he had lost his job, he had much to be thankful for.

No longer in a stressful working environment, he found his health improved, and his relationship with his family flourished. He adopted the Golden Rule and forgave as he had been forgiven. Now he focuses on the presence of God in his life and is confident of His leading.

I like to recall the story about David and Goliath. Everyone was afraid of Goliath because he seemed unconquerable and invincible. When other people ran away in fear, young David didn't concede. Instead, he confronted the giant in faith, despite his frightening appearance.

Although David was a small shepherd boy with only a slingshot and a pouch of stones to face down a huge armored villain, he believed God would give him the strength to defeat his opponent.

Confident that his Lord was with him, David shouted to the Philistine,

> You come to me with a sword, with a spear, and with a javelin. But I come to you in the name of the LORD of hosts, the God of the armies of Israel, whom you have defied. This day the LORD will deliver you into my hand, . . . that all the earth may know that there is a God in Israel. . . . The LORD does not save with sword and spear; for the battle is the LORD's, and He will give you into our hands.
>
> (1 Samuel 17:45–47 NKJV)

As Goliath, scoffing, moved in to destroy David, the young shepherd boy reached into his bag, pulled out a stone, and slung it straight at Goliath's head. Miraculously, the small stone found its way through a hole in Goliath's armor, hit his forehead, and knocked him to the ground, never to rise again.

Today, if you are being unfairly treated and you feel helpless, boldly say as David did, "This battle is the Lord's!"

When I was in my late teens, I was onstage performing a ballet routine from the musical *Oklahoma*. Suddenly, in the middle of the performance, there were technical problems and the music just *stopped*. But I kept on dancing!

If your music stops for a time, keep on dancing! Don't sit in fear. Carry on in faith.

Realize that nothing can overcome the will of our all-powerful, all-loving God. Scripture says, "The LORD will fight for you, and you shall hold your peace" (Exodus 14:14 NKJV). He is with you, He will battle for you, and He will lead the way to a succession of greater victories.

FORGIVENESS WILL OPEN UNEXPECTED DOORS

There is a Force beyond what we can see, a Supreme Power at work in our lives. I read in 2 Corinthians 12 how the apostle Paul suffered from a "thorn in the flesh." No matter what the "thorn" was, it caused Paul to suffer. Scripture records Paul saying, "Three different times I begged the Lord to take it away" (2 Corinthians 12:8 NIV).

But instead of taking away the ordeal, God said to Paul, "My grace is sufficient for you, for my power is made perfect in weakness" (2 Corinthians 12:9 NIV).

Every setback, problem, or disappointment is an opportunity in disguise . . . for it holds within it great lessons and even greater gifts.

I know a woman who was wronged in the workplace. She was a leader in her community, honest and hardworking. However, there was resentment from others on the job and a desire to see her defeated. A whispering campaign was begun against her, and finally she had to resign, leaving behind her company health insurance, her high salary, and her self-confidence.

Embittered, she questioned her faith in her fellow man, and then she began to doubt the Lord she had always believed in. In her despair, though, she happened to read this verse: "I make *all things* new" (Revelations 21:5 NKJV). God was still with her, still working in her life. A new sense of freedom enveloped her.

The woman gave thanks to God for His presence in her life. Then she felt moved to forgive everyone who had hurt her. From that moment on, she saw her life change dramatically. Her resentment fell away, and her heart began to open toward others once again.

Today, she runs her own successful corporation, doing what she loves best—serving as a corporate consultant to show other company owners how to get the best from their staff members by treating them like the treasures they truly are. Her reputation is stellar, she is paid an excellent salary, and she is living a life she never dreamed possible.

God brought her the lessons of humility and sensitivity toward others; He turned the pain she had experienced into greater good for herself and others. Indeed, He made "all things new"!

WE ALL HAVE THE SAME PARENT—A LOVING GOD

After my mother passed away, I carried with me feelings of inadequacy. Rejected, scared, and depressed, I had no parent figure upon whom I could rely, and there was no one I trusted enough to give me advice or direction.

Does anyone truly care? I often asked myself. I began to believe I wasn't worthy of love.

The answer to those questions came to me over eighteen years ago in four simple words. One Saturday morning, I met an acquaintance for breakfast, a sweet, smiling, white-haired woman I had known from church.

She knew a bit about my life, but I am sure she was able to read between the lines. Compassionately, she told me that I was loved and cherished, and that God had a great plan for my life. Listening to her words, I desperately wanted to believe that she was right. *Maybe God hasn't forgotten me. . . . Maybe He has been with me all along.* Gratefully, I rested my hand next to hers.

"Catherine," she said gently, almost like an angel ministering to my sadness, "*God is your Father.*"

I was taken aback by her statement, not understanding at first. And then it was as if a dazzling, intense light had been switched on in a pitch-black room.

I now understood—everything!

I knew that God was my true Father and that He loved me, despite everything I had gone through. This knowledge let me unleash all my past hurts, guilt, and rejection, and I could see the dawning of a brighter tomorrow. Actually, I saw that *every* tomorrow had the potential to be brighter!

The meaning of that sweet woman's words helped to change the course of my thinking—and ultimately my life. And through the years, I have passed on those four words to many other lost souls who need to believe in, and then receive, God's love.

Maybe you, too, are shouldering guilt and were betrayed or cast down. Perhaps you lost one parent or both. If so, commit this to memory: *God is my Father.*

One important key to obtaining your heart's desire is to realize how valuable you are and how much you are loved by God. He doesn't create failures or mistakes; He guides your steps and leads you to joy, even though your path may be littered with obstacles. Remember, you are His much-loved child, just as Jesus was—His prized possession.

Stand tall and be proud. If God can order the galaxies and stars to stay on their courses and make the human heart and mind the most complex of wonders, then He can restore and rebuild all things in and around you.

He is the master Fixer, so you must read His Book and trust in Him. You can't read it and obey it and not be changed. Be patient with yourself; carry on with head held high, heart humbled, and trust, trust, trust.

Believe in Him, and one day you, too, will stand in awe to see what a masterpiece He has made of your life.

GOD, GRANT ME THE SERENITY . . .

Life hits hard sometimes.

Perhaps you have encountered an unforeseen setback, your present circumstances appear uncertain, even your prayers seem to go unanswered. And maybe you are full of anxiety.

But if you stand firm, you will find deliverance in the Lord. He will sweep away the disappointments of the past and bring you to a place of peace, for victories are not born of good times. They're born out of trials.

A short time ago, I received a letter from a remarkable young woman who has breast cancer. After her diagnosis, the man who had been in her life for years decided to end the relationship.

She was devastated and felt more alone than ever before. But her heart was a loving one, and she couldn't feel resentment for long.

And so she forgave this man, understanding that he had left her because he could not stand seeing her life in jeopardy. He felt helpless and unable to contribute to her survival. And so he fled.

She realized that she could not rely on anyone other than God to see her through her difficulty. As she has moved through the process of healing, she has kept her heart and mind in a peaceful state by surrounding herself with good people and expecting to come through her trials successfully. While others marvel at her capacity to forgive and move forward, she wrote to me, "I know that I have many blessings in my life, and they are far greater than the bumps in the road of life. I just keep looking forward to new beginnings."

Often things happen to us that we simply cannot fathom. Instead of holding on to anxiety and doubting God's fairness, though, our reaction should be: "If God be for us, who can be against us?" (Romans 8:31 KJV). "No weapon formed against [us] shall prosper" (Isaiah 54:17 NKJV). "God is with [us] in all that [we] do" (Genesis 21:22 NKJV).

Then, surrender the situation to God. Remember, He guided Joseph to store up food for seven years of famine. He can certainly provide you with your daily bread of life.

A Midwestern gentleman e-mailed me, describing the extreme economic circumstances in his state. Bankruptcies and home foreclosures were occurring more frequently than ever before. Encouraged by my column to wait on the Lord, this man reflected on Job, who faced unthinkable loss but maintained his belief in God's sovereignty. In the end, he noted, God restored twice what Job had lost.

The book of Job in the Bible describes how Job didn't understand why God had permitted such afflictions and tribulations to come to him, as he had been an upright man. Job suffered terribly, losing his family, his health, and his worldly goods. He despaired. He was angry at God and accused Him of denying him justice. Finally he challenged God in a duel of words . . . and lost. The Bible says, "Then the LORD answered Job out of the storm. He said, 'Who is this that darkens my counsel with words without knowledge?'" (Job 38:1–2 NIV).

Through his scores of trials, Job learned valuable lessons and trusted in the will of God. And by the end of his story, as this reader from the Midwest described, God restored to Job twice as much as he had lost and brought Job blessings in the latter part of Job's life to compensate for the trials in his earlier years.

In our front yard garden we have a lovely stepping-stone engraved with the Serenity Prayer: "God, grant me the serenity to accept the things I cannot change, courage to change the things I can, and wisdom to know the difference." These words, from theologian Reinhold Niebuhr, always remind me that a sense of serenity is indeed a gift from God, available to us whenever we need it. Just knowing this, I feel that I can face whatever situation might loom up before me.

SEEK GOD'S LOVE IN THE WORLD AROUND YOU

Climbing a sand bank and gazing out over the beach, I heard the lightly gusting winds, the cry of seagulls, and the pounding of the sea. . . . The beach was almost deserted as a lone airplane circled overhead.

The eastern sky was a clear sapphire blue, with just a fragment of white clouds. And if I listened intently, I could even hear the rasp of the breeze off the dune grasses nestled atop a gently rising slope.

Listening to nature's music, the progression of the waves, the melody of children's gleeful voices, and the murmur of gentle breezes, I sat down in the sand and let my thoughts drift.

I watched as the grasses of the field bent with the wind. Then I pondered, *Which force is stronger: that which comes against us, or the ability to humbly bend and let it go by?*

Taking a deep breath, I walked to the ocean's edge, where the waves progressively washed upon the fawn-colored sand. I bent down and picked up a dark, smooth pebble. On bended knee, with the stone, I wrote a few words in the sand about a situation that had been bothering me. . . .

Then, as quickly as the blink of an eye, the surf rolled in and washed away my words.

You may have suffered, endured hardships, and had difficulties to handle. But no matter how many setbacks you have endured, know this: they are over and done. Today is a new day, a defining moment. What happened long ago is history, and with forgiveness in your heart, right now, at this very second, you can start anew.

I know that life can be full of situations that try to steal your joy. Do you want to let that happen? What are you allowing to upset you? Is it worth spoiling the wonder of this precious day?

A petty annoyance, an unjust criticism, or a barrier in your path should not hold you back from the joy of *this* day. Scripture says, "*This is the day* the LORD has made; let us rejoice and be glad in it" (Psalm 118:24 NIV, italics added). So make the most of and enjoy each moment, and let serenity, contentment, and joy govern your heart.

How you handle every circumstance will determine your peace. Do you want to approach life as a creator or a pessimist, a conqueror or a prisoner? Do you want to be full of kindness or full of cruelty? Are you a giver or a taker?

You cannot change what others unjustly try to do to you,

their spiteful actions, jealous natures, or what someone hurtfully says. Although you'd probably like to, you can't change a person. As with the weather, you can't do anything but accept what comes. If people want to change, they must do so themselves.

However, you can pray for those who have hurt you, because if you bless them instead of curse them, it is you who will be free. I recall the Scripture that says, "When you stand praying, if you hold anything against anyone, forgive him, so that your Father in heaven may forgive you your sins" (Mark 11:25 NIV).

Search your heart several times a day, and if something is disturbing your peace, focus on restoring yourself to calm. Whenever my cares threaten to overwhelm me, I call to mind that peaceful time I spent at the beach, as I knelt beneath the canopy of God's azure sky.

As if I were still there, I can almost hear the murmurs of the surf, the warm whispering breeze. Then I can begin to feel the healing progression to calm as I shift my awareness from the fast pace of daily life to the sweet balm of that oceanside moment.

I remember how I was moved to write down my problem in the sand and softly voice a prayer. And I remember how my heart felt as cleansed as the sand when the tide came in and washed my worry away, into my heavenly Father's care.

I strolled back to my car, tranquil, contented, renewed.

And I did not look back.

FORGIVENESS:
Key to Your Heart's Desire

○—🔑 Whom will you forgive today? When you show mercy, grace, and compassion toward another in the Lord's name, no matter what else you may achieve in your lifetime, that understanding will follow you all the way from earth to heaven.

○—🔑 Problems are a part of life. So forgive yourself for past mistakes, forgive others for hurting you, and never quit. Persevere and press on.

○—🔑 Turn your trials over to God. For if He could part the Red Sea so that the children of Israel could walk across on dry land, He can certainly deliver you from your troubles. But you must remember . . . the children of Israel had to get up and walk. You also have to get up and move forward.

○—🔑 If someone hurts you, play it down. Do not dwell on it. You have heard the saying "Don't burn your bridges." You'll be amazed how many times you will cross that same river.

∘—🔑   Don't hold grudges or resentment. Ignore faults, concentrate on what is good. You can't change a person by enumerating his or her faults.

∘—🔑   Stop finding fault with yourself. Everyone has weaknesses, so when you are tempted to criticize yourself, say something constructive instead. Forgive yourself for small things; know that God created you in His image to excel, to achieve, and to enjoy your life.

∘—🔑   Today is the first day of the rest of your life: a time of glorious new beginnings has arrived. Give thanks for your blessings, and bring love and forgiveness to all who deserve it—everyone and everything created by God.

Afterword

It's been said, "Life is a book, and there are sections within." Everything has a chapter, a time, a beginning . . . and an end.

Although this book has come to an end, it is only the start of wonderful things for you.

Today I am at the beach near our home with my three young daughters playing cheerfully along the edge of the cool water. I'm filled with love and thankfulness as I pass on these words to you.

My prayer is that with these seven keys in hand, you will create the life that God wants you to live, a life of faith, persistence, optimism, hope, gratitude, love, and forgiveness. And I hope that these keys will help you, as they have helped me, to achieve your heart's desires.

Each precious day, "you shall go out in joy, and be led forth in peace; the mountains and the hills before you shall break forth into singing, and all the trees of the field shall clap their hands" (Isaiah 55:12 RSV).

God loves you, and so do I.

Blessings,

Catherine

About the Author

CATHERINE GALASSO-VIGORITO's nationally syndicated weekly column, "A New You," has endeared her to readers worldwide for over fifteen years. Known for her ability to uplift and encourage, Catherine has become America's most beloved inspirational voice. In addition to her newspaper column, she has appeared on TV and radio, bringing her message of encouragement to millions of people around the world. Catherine is founder and CEO of her own company, A New You Worldwide, developing and designing inspirational products. Her mission is to instill hope in the hearts of people everywhere, inspiring them to a better life. Catherine lives in a quiet New England town with her husband, Todd, and their three daughters. You can learn more about her at www.anewyouworldwide.com.